VAMPIRE

THE MASQUERADE

REDEMPTION

By Siôn Rodriguez y Gibson

BRADYGAMES

TAKE YOUR GAME FURTHER™

VAMPIRE: THE MASQUERADE® - REDEMPTION™
Official Strategy Guide

LEGAL STUFF

Brady Publishing
An Imprint of
Macmillan USA, Inc.
201 W. 103rd St.
Indianapolis, IN 46290

ISBN: 1-56686-980-3
Library of Congress No.: 00-13447

Printing Code: The rightmost double-digit number is the year of the book's printing; the rightmost single-digit number is the number of the book's printing. For example, 00-1 shows that the first printing of the book occurred in 2000.

03 02 01 00   4 3 2 1

BradyGAMES Staff

Editor-In-Chief	H. Leigh Davis
Director of Business Development	David Waybright
Licensing Assistant	Mike Degler
Creative Director	Robin Lasek
Marketing Manager	Janet Eshenour
Marketing Assistant	Tricia Reynolds

Credits

Project Editor	David B. Bartley
Screenshot Editor	Michael Owen
Book Designer	Kurt Owens
Production Designers	Jane Washburne Lisa England Bob Klunder
Indexer	Johnna VanHoose Dinse

About the Author

Siôn Rodriguez y Gibson would like to describe himself as an olde worlde monster. A recent migrant to the New World, he has undertaken more temporary positions than most people have had hot dinners, before settling into the gaming industry. As a result of all those past jobs, he can pull a pint, break up a fight, and fix a killer cappuccino.

Should you ever meet him, bribing him with a pint of Guinness is a good way to hear more than you ever wanted to know about vampires and their cousins in darkness.

He makes his lair in the City of Angels.

Acknowledgments

To Liza, for keeping me out of the noonday sun.

To White Wolf for giving me a chance to write in such a glorious fictional world.

To Activision for keeping me off the streets.

To the editors at Brady, for Americanizing my spelling.

And to everyone whose mother ever said "Stop playing those stupid games and get a real job!"

Contents

Introduction: A Cavalcade of Monsters

I never believed that they would come for me. Sure, I'd heard rumors that this wasn't just a game, that it was real, but I didn't believe them. I mean this is almost the twenty-first century and it's a video game about vampires! Seriously!

Of course they came at night, they always come at night. When I answered the door and there were the three people standing there, I assumed they had the wrong house. I was about to tell them to try next door when the woman smiled and I saw her teeth. This is LA, I'm used to surgery and artificially perfect people, but there was something different in her face. Even the kinkiest rich person doesn't pay for fangs, not when they're razor sharp and gleaming in the moonlight.

"You will come with us," were the first words I heard out of a vampire's mouth. I guess that's how most of them deal with us, giving commands, expecting obedience. I started to protest, but then found myself unable to speak. If I hadn't been shaking I could not have moved at all. Her smile grew wider and I lost myself in her violet eyes.

"Anatole, Becket, get his laptop. Check for any disks and remember to get the hardcopy this time." Her accent was vaguely European, smoothed over by years of travelling. The woman's companions pushed their way past me and I heard them moving through my apartment. In a few moments they emerged carrying my laptop, notes, and a bundle of disks.

"Follow me!" she said, and I did, helpless as a child. I wanted to object that this was wrong, that they didn't exist, that they had left my apartment door open. As they pushed me into their car, a black limousine, I knew that I had left my world behind. I had entered the World of Darkness.

I entered the World of Darkness for the first time in 1991 when I noticed a new game book at the local store. It had a green marble cover and a cool title, *Vampire The Masquerade*. I flicked through it looking at the pictures and barely registering the strange names and words: Diablerie, Brujah, Camarilla, Anathema, and Masquerade. I gladly handed over my dollars to the shop owner. I read the book for the first time that night and stepped across the threshold into another world.

This new world, the World of Darkness, was like a dark reflection of ours, one of those mirror universes where everyone has a goatee and wears bondage gear. I played in games, ran a few, and even dressed up in my best clubbing gear to try live-action. I was hooked—I had (if you will forgive me) been bitten. There were rumors there was to be a computer game, but no one believed them. White Wolf was a little company, computer games were all first person shooters, and no one could possibly want to play a story game as a vampire.

Skip forward a few years. *Fallout* and *Baldur's Gate* put computer roleplaying games back on the map. TSR had gone bankrupt and been bought by a little company that made a card game. White Wolf was now one of the largest pen-and-paper gaming companies and the World of Darkness had expanded up to five core books. Now talk of a computer game didn't seem so far fetched.

Deals were struck and a new company Nihilistic, with some of the big names in the business (check their bios if you don't believe me), was contracted to bring the game to life. They were ambitious; not only would the game bring the World of Darkness to life, but it would have a single player story that covered eight centuries, as well as a multiplayer mode that allowed Storytellers to do everything they could in the tabletop game.

No one really believed any of this until E3 (the gaming industry's big exhibition in which all the latest and hottest games and hardware are first demo'd). People saw the screenshots, the concept art, and even got to play a small section of the game and they were hooked. Now people were talking about *Vampire* and beginning to look forward to it.

> *They had style; I'll admit that. I expected some grimy warehouse and a scene out of a bad gangster movie. Instead, they took me to a house up in the Hollywood hills overlooking the city. One thing was certain: they didn't care if I knew where they lived, err, where they made their haven I mean, so that meant I wasn't walking out of there alive. The house looked like the set of a cheap porno movie. Perhaps it was. They control the porn business, don't they? They took me to a room, '70s shag carpet and wall-to-wall mirrors, and locked the door, leaving me alone with my laptop and my thoughts.*

Now, as I write this, E3 is almost upon us again. This time Nihilistic (and Activision, the game's publisher) won't be showing a demo. They will be showing an almost complete version. Pretty soon after that, everyone will see what the fuss has been about when the game is released to the public.

I've been involved with the game since late autumn of last year. Working as part of Activision's QA test team, I've played the game for almost six months. I've been up to Nihilistic's offices in northern California and read the sign outside their office that solicitors will be hung up and tapped—strange guys! (I always wondered if they meant solicitors, as in people trying to sell them things, or solicitor in the English usage, which means lawyers. Jonathan Harker was a solicitor.) I saw Ecaterina's University before the words of Caine were carved into the walls. I've played guessing games with the artists as to which famous works of arts had been stolen and hung on the walls of havens and secret societies in London.

> *I had always thought Jonathan Harker in Bram Stoker's Dracula was a wuss. He scarcely tried to escape the castle even after it was patently obvious that he was being held prisoner by a vampire. Now I know better. As the night passed I could hear my captors moving around the house. Sometimes their voices were raised in argument, other times they were as quiet as cats. But as the sky lightened outside, I knew they must sleep and I could escape. I started to get up, then stopped and slumped back down on the bed. I wanted to get up; I wanted to smash the window and escape, but I could not. The thought of escape made me tired, hope drained away, and I watched the light move slowly across the carpet hour-by-hour until it faded and it was night again.*

Now the game is almost finished. I've played through it more times than I can count, gradually refining my tactics and knowledge of the game until it is nearly perfect. If the world described in the game were real, I would be at home there. And that is the wonderful thing about this game. It contains worlds, not just a single story. The single player game is enthralling and leads to speculations: What would have happened if I had made a different choice there? What happened to Serena? Did she fall with her clan or could she possibly be alive somewhere? What did Wilhem do over the eight centuries while Christof slept? These are all the side stories contained within the single plot arc of *Redemption*.

There is a moment in the creation of a video game, especially a roleplaying or adventure game, when the characters stop being numbers or animations and become people. This happened a few months ago in the development. Suddenly members of the team were talking about the characters as people and taking the game seriously. We knew then we had reached a threshold and could look forward to the time that the game was complete.

> *The woman entered my room alone. She was wearing a tight evening dress and there was what looked like blood under her fingernails. She regarded me silently and then walked over to me. I saw that though I was reflected a dozen times in the mirrors, she cast no reflection. I think I began laughing at that moment, a high wild sound.*
>
> *"Sssshhh!" She placed her fingertip on my lips and I was silent. "You know we will kill you, that much is certain. But it does not have to be hard. We do not wish to hurt you." I could not speak. I could only stare up at her, wondering what I seemed like to her. A frightened animal? Food? Nothing?*
>
> *"Soon we will ask you questions and you will answer them. But we need to investigate other leads first. Before long, it will all be over, we need you for but a short time." She ran her fingernail down the edge of my cheek, pressing hard, then took it to her own wrist. Blood fountained up, deep rich crimson, and she pressed it to my lips.*
>
> *"Take this; it will sustain you until we need you."*

In some ways, you, the new player of the game, are in an enviable position. You did not see the game when it was unfinished—when art, disciplines, and even characters were missing. And you have no idea what to expect when the great opening movie plays. This guide does reveal all the secrets and surprises. It tells you about the enemies you will face and the powers you have at your command to defeat them. If you use it wisely, you will only dip into it when you need it, rather than sitting down and reading it cover to cover. Do that *after* you have completed the game once— see if you missed any secrets, see if it gives you any ideas for when you play the game again.

And you will play the game again. *Redemption* presents a deep and rich world. The second time you play, play more slowly. Use first person mode (hold down Z) to look around. Check out the carvings and painting on the walls, see what a szlachta looks like close up. Take the path less traveled and see what's there.

The next day I woke with a raging thirst, but the thought of water repelled me. I knew what I needed and it disgusted me. I had to do something. They had left me my laptop, and I looked over my notes thinking of ways to fight vampires, thinking of a way to fight a vampire that had me in her thrall.

My laptop! If there was a phone line in the room, I could get a message out. Searching, I found one, but whom could I contact? The police would not believe my story, wouldn't come up the hill to this rich neighborhood just because of an email. My friends would think it was a joke. Who could I call?

If they had found me through my contract with BradyGAMES, a contract hammered out over the phone and through email, perhaps they were watching the Internet. Busy little search engines looking for breaches in the Masquerade, looking for humans who knew. Perhaps, then, other vampires were watching, too— vampires like Dev/Null with the knowledge and skill to shift the data of the human world, looking for the anomalies. Perhaps someone would notice.

I began posting my plea for salvation across the news groups and message boards, hoping someone would hear me.

Beyond the single player game, which is detailed here, there are the vast possibilities for the multiplayer game. Nihilistic has created a toolkit for creating your own adventures and handed it to you. This is perhaps a first in computer roleplaying games. The design tools they used to make the world of *Redemption* are available to you nightly. Through WON you can meet opponents, make friends, and tell your own stories.

The skills you have learned playing the single player chronicle will serve you well in multiplayer games. You will know the secrets of Damned existence, the ins and outs of discipline use, and the wars between the clans. With this knowledge you can create stories of your own, continue Christof's adventures, and find out what happened across the missing centuries.

"I am Christof Romuald, I was a man of God and a soldier in Heaven's cause. Now, and forever, I am one of the Damned. But I am the last Promethean and we do not abuse humans." A tall man had entered my room, not one of my captors, but not a stranger, either.

9

He took my hand and pulled me to my feet, his strong grip steadying me as I almost fell. I stared up into a face that I knew well, that I had thought was merely a character in a game.

"No one else should die so that my story be told. I pray thee send this to your editors and have done with it. Once it has been published, there is nothing they can do; you will be in no more danger." He picked up my laptop and scrolled down the document open on the desktop. He laughed once, "You have captured the gist of it, if not the spirit! Still, it is good to be remembered."

He handed the laptop back to me.

I'm wrapping this up here because you don't want to be reading the words of someone who has already been there; you want to get into the game and go there yourself. Good luck, use the information in this book wisely and you may face the Voivode.

If you survive that encounter, look me up online… there is always room for another childe of Caine in the World of Darkness.

I stepped into the pre-dawn light, palm trees silhouetted against the neon sky, and breathed the air. The smoggy hum of traffic was muted in the distance and I stared out over the City of Angels. I clutched my laptop to my chest and began to walk down the hill toward Sunset Boulevard. I would find a cybercafe, send off my manuscript, and drink a double latte.

Then, then I would walk back up the hill in the sunlight and search for the basement, or the cellar, or the darkened room where my captors slept. You see I'd tasted vampire blood, and I couldn't go back to late nights sustained only by coffee after that.

— Siôn Rodriguez y Gibson
May 2000

Walkthrough

Your adventure in *Vampire: The Masquerade - Redemption* will take you through Prague, Vienna, London, and New York City, as well as various time periods throughout the course of history. Each setting presents its own unique challenges and quests, including a host of unique beasts to battle.

Our story begins in Medieval Prague, and so does the walkthrough strategy portion of this guide. Good luck!

Prague

Before beginning the detailed strategy of the Prague segment of your adventure, let's briefly discuss each area you'll encounter.

Starting Out

The opening scene is intended to begin after the cutscene intro, showing Anezka and Christof within the Convent. The Convent is under attack by raiding szlachta. Christof awakens and defends the nuns. Kill the szlachta attacking Anezka and her chubby sister. After the battle, Christof falls from the pain of his battle wound. He awakens and talks with Anezka. Here you will have a conversational decision (click on the response). The Archbishop interrupts and the scene ends.

Silver Mines

The next scene begins with Christof all dressed up and ready to go out to the mines. From here you can visit Jiri and Unorna and explore most of Prague before heading out the east gate to the mines (near the University). Journey through the mines to meet Ahzra at the bottom. Kill her and return to Prague.

The Becoming

Christof gets lovey-dovey and gives Anezka the locket before being interrupted by the Archbishop. Heading outside, it's "Prague by Night." Run over to the clock tower, then run back, kill the ghouls, and enter the Convent. Kill all the baddies—Ecaterina is around the corner awaiting the embrace.

Nod Fragment

Head over to Petrin Hill Monastery (several small conversations here). Traverse to the bottom level and you'll find the bone key, which can be used to enter Garinol's study. Go to the back of the room (near Garinol's bed) and find the Lamia Skull. Use the skull to enter Mercurio's study, then confront him and retrieve the fragment. Return up to the outside of the monastery. From here, we get the Anezka visit scene, followed by the debriefing at the University.

Golem

The coterie has learned of Mercurio's treachery, and the out-of-control golem. They head out to the northern quarter and find Mendel, who tells them the secret to killing the golem. Head under the arch and into the destroyed area, then kill the golem, retrieve the Shem, and return it to Mendel. At this point you can meet Garinol (at Petrin Hill) to give him the Shem and gain Serena. Afterwards, go back to the University or Unorna's shop to learn of Anezka's disappearance. When you enter your haven, you get a cutscene with Serena. Later, Christof decides to visit the Prince.

Reliquary

The Prince scene describes the reliquary mission. The party then must visit Josef to gain access to his tunnels. (You need to visit Josef, then return to Ecaterina at the University to get her vitae.) Return to Josef and enter his tunnels. You must make your way over to the labyrinth under St. Vitus' cathedral (find the secret exit back up to Golden Lane), retrieve the reliquary, and return to the Prince. The Prince tells of Ardan's chantry and the secret Tremere infiltration to Prague. Christof decides to storm the chantry and hopefully find Anezka.

Ardan's Chantry

Go to Ardan's Chantry on Golden Lane (house at the end of the lane, with trees growing through it). Enter the back entrance and walk down the stairway. At the bottom of the chantry, you'll find Erik, freeing him so he'll join the party. Walk to the next area and meet/battle Ardan. So ends the Prague chronicle, you'll transition to Vienna after a cutscene at the University and leaving via the East Gate.

Welcome to Vienna

The coterie appears at Vienna's northern gate, near a desecrated church (your haven for this hub). Enter the door to the Ringstrasse (the circular road that encompasses the city). Head to the right and enter the eastern door to the marketplace. The green building is the Green Frog Inn. Enter there and talk to one of the triplets. You'll receive an invitation to Count Orsi's party. (You can also visit the Order of Hermes magic shop run by Orvus at this point.)

Stephansdom

Exit back onto the Ringstrasse and head west. To the far west, there is a gate to Orsi's mansion. Enter and talk to the triplets again. Orsi will introduce himself and give you the Luther Black quest. Exit back onto the Ringstrasse and head straight into the Innerstrasse (area in the middle of the ring). There is a board that allows you to climb the buildings and enter through an open window. From here you can climb up and back out along rooftops until you reach the face of the astronomical clock. Click on the door and enter. Make your way through the secret entrance to the church and find Luther (at the top of the tower). After talking to him, a door to the upper area is opened. There you will find two switches that must be activated within five seconds of each other (use two party members in Out of Party mode or one with Celerity pumped up). After the death sequence, head back down the stairs you ascended. You'll meet Orsi, and will then be teleported to the dungeons of the Deutschordenskirche.

Teutonic Knight Base

Cast Potence on one of your party characters and use your added strength to open the door to your cell. Battle your way upstairs and kill the Tremere on the next level up. He will drop an amulet. Take this and get out of the base.

Haus de Hexe

Go back to the marketplace in the Eastern Ringstrasse and enter the other building there—the Order of Hermes. Talk to Orvus who will charge the amulet to allow entry into the Haus de Hexe. Go out to the southern Ringstrasse and through the gates into the Haus. This level has three branches, each will deliver an Arcanulum piece used to open the main door to Etrius' chamber. Once you have all three pieces, click on the triangular image in the main room, and go back upstairs to talk with Etrius (picking up the Journal initiates these events). Erik will be transformed. Fight the Gargoyle, then battle Etrius. Take the Journal back to Orvus and then exit Vienna through the north gate (by your haven). You'll be transported back to Prague, which is partially destroyed due to the outbreak of the war between the Tremere and Tzimisce, and the uprising of the mortals.

Prague2: Devil's Night

Enter the door leading to Vysehrad castle (near the convent). Progress down through the pantry until you reach Vukodlak's resting place. After the conversation with Anezka, the house falls down and you proceed to the modern day act.

Prague by Day

Prologue

Christof awakens in the convent. Rising from bed, he grasps his sword and responds to the disturbance in the next room. Here you find two szlachta menacing Anezka. Kill the szlachta to continue.

Kill the szlachta.

Battling Szlachta

Szlachta are twisted products of vampire evil. Once normal creatures, or even people, they have been twisted by the discipline of Vicissitude into these shambling monsters. Although they appear clumsy and slow moving, they can be deadly opponents in groups.

After the fight, Christof collapses. Upon regaining consciousness, speak with Sister Anezka and Archbishop Geza with bravery, not cowardice, or you will lose humanity.

Gaining and Losing Humanity

Your humanity trait is a measure of your personal honor, self-worth, and the integrity of your soul. Most mortals can maintain a semblance of humanity no matter what sins they commit (though they can be plagued by guilt or even madness). To a vampire humanity is even more important as without this hold on their mortality they gradually slip into delusions and insanity—the embrace of the Beast—until they become twisted mockeries like Ahzra. You can lose humanity by committing evil acts or making immoral choices. During the game you face many such choices and your humanity will rise or fall by the responses you make!

Receive Quest : Reclaim the Bonn Silver Mines

16

Primus: The Next Morning on the Streets of Prague

Golden Prague is a medieval city on the verge of Renaissance. It will become fabled in later years as a center of learning and culture in Eastern Europe, partially due to your actions within the game. For now, most of Prague is brick and wood with muddy streets running between the gabled buildings. A few buildings show what the city will look like in later years—the University and vast castles on the fringes of town.

As the game begins, Christof is awake and fully dressed in the convent. You can talk to Anezka (she will heal you if you are wounded) or leave the convent immediately. Outside are the streets of Prague, a bustling medieval town only just feeling the touch of evil.

There are several optional encounters before you leave for the mines:

Knights of St. John	Opposite convent. Will talk to Christof. Flavor text.
Jiri the Weaponsmith	Will buy/sell armor and weapons. Also can give location of Unorna.
Unorna the Wise Woman	Has information on vampires. Buy/sell magic items.

Exploring Prague

Prague is a fairly small town and you should be able to find your way by using the map, but it does have a few secrets. Several of the townsfolk will talk to you providing information that will help you on your quest. Also, there are breakable barrels around the place—two opposite the convent, two outside Jiri's shop, and two facing the University. These can provide rusty weapons and basic salves.

Once you leave the Convent, the door to St. Thomas' Cathedral is immediately ahead and to the right. You can enter the Cathedral to receive Archbishop Geza's blessing.

Experience Bonuses

Several actions in the game win you an experience bonus, many through making the 'correct' choices in conversations. This encounter with the Archbishop is one such incident. If he does bless you, you receive a small experience award; however, if you avoid this meeting, you do not get it.

Leave the Cathedral and go to where the two Knights of St. John (your Sword brethren) are guarding the intersection. Talk to them, and then continue down the road. On your left is the Inn of Four Stags where you can talk to the Barkeep, but you don't have time to drink!

At the next intersection, past the Inn, turning right takes you to the Cathedral and Eastgate, while turning left takes you to Jiri the Blacksmith and Judith Bridge. Turn right, passing under the clock tower, then continue to the building adjacent to the stables—this is Jiri's.

Visit Jiri the blacksmith and purchase a torch—you'll need it in the dark mines.

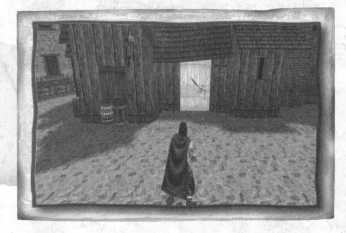

Entering Jiri's smithy and talk to him. He will question you about your mission and you can choose how you treat this humble man. This is a test of Christof's morality—all options lead the same way, but if you are polite and non-bigoted, Jiri gives you information about Unorna. Jiri's merchant screen opens. Sell any trash you picked up, then buy a torch and armor if you can afford it. Jiri will buy any weapons and armor you find on your travels.

Merchants

When you visit a merchant, a new screen will open with your inventory on the right and the merchant's stock on the left. If you highlight items in your inventory, the price that you are being offered will appear on the merchant's screen. Press the sell button if you want to sell your selection at that price. If you highlight an item in stock, its price will appear and you can select the Buy button if you want to purchase it. Rollover text will appear for items in the merchant's stock, so you can decide if it is useful to you.

When you leave Jiri's, you can see the alleyway that leads onto Judith Bridge. Follow it and cross the bridge. At the open space at the end, you have a choice of directions:

Left	Petrin Hill (Petrin Hill Monastery)
Straight	Prague Castle (Prince Brandl's chambers)
Right	Golden Lane (Unorna's shop and Ardan's Chantry)

Go right onto Golden Lane. Unorna's shop is in clear view (it has flames burning outside it). Unorna is a wise woman who can tell you much lore about vampires. She will also buy and sell any mystical items you find on your quest. (Ardan's Chantry is at the top of Golden Lane and the exit from the Tunnels is halfway up; both are sealed at this point.)

Stop by Unorna's shop on Golden lane.

After talking to Unorna, go back over the bridge, then turn left and approach the University, a large white building. Prague's East Gate is to the right. You can talk to the old man who waits by the gate before you leave town.

The two knights guarding the gate mock you. Ignore their taunts and follow the path between the boulders to the mine entrance. Abandoned carts surround the entrance to the mine and, as you enter the tunnel, the sunlight fades behind you.

Bonn Silver Mines

Enemies	Ghoul rats, rat leaders, szlachta, boss szlachta, war ghouls
Boss	Ahzra the Unliving
Treasures	Silver Shield, Amulet of St. Jude
Quests	Reclaim the Bonn Silver Mines

Overview

The mines are divided into three levels. The first is a very worked section showing many signs of excavations—as you venture deeper, the mines get wetter and darker with more natural rock formations and twisty passages. As you progress further into the mines, the enemies are also stronger and there are more signs of their master's work. The level ends with a confrontation with Ahzra the Unliving in her blasphemous cathedral.

General Tactics

Attack systematically. The creatures in the mines (szlachta and rats) are pack creatures and will easily overwhelm Christof. However, they are greedy and individualistic, so they can be lured out of groups if you're careful. Never run into a room. Instead, stand at the threshold and coax them out with the smell of your blood. If one catches the scent, it will come toward you on its own without alerting its comrades. This strategy enables you to defeat a group by breaking it down!

Play conservatively. Carry a torch to light your way, but always equip a shield and stand ready to fight whenever you hear or see danger approaching.

Listen carefully. You can hear both rats and szlachta from a distance. Learn to interpret the sounds beyond the sounds of water and listen for your foes. Hearing them approach you gives you enough time to prepare.

Don't be afraid to retreat. At this stage of the game you are only human and can die as easily as any other mortal. If you run out of healing salves and are wounded or overwhelmed, return to town. Sister Anezka can heal you and you may have collected enough loot to buy armor from Jiri.

Navigating the Mines

Overall, the mines present a fairly straightforward level. Generally speaking, a single path connects a series of larger chambers. Unless you get confused and turned around, you should have no difficulty moving through the dungeon. If you do get lost, pay attention to the details of individual rooms so that you will know if you've been there before. Notice mine carts, stalagmites, and pools of water, which can help you to get your bearings.

Level 1: Abandoned Mine

The upper levels of the mines are hewn from soft, green sandstone. The veins of silver here are mostly exhausted, but work continued until the Tzimisce overran the mines. You can see the abandoned tools of the miners and even a few poor souls who were not lucky enough to escape. There are pools of stagnant water and some rock falls, but this level of the mines is in overall good repair.

Follow the narrow path into the mines and you will pass several barricaded doors. One of these will be open when you complete the quest, so you can return quickly to the surface. As you follow a path over a deep drop, you can see the lower depths of the mines.

Stairs lead deeper underground, and as you reach the bottom of the stairs you notice a dead body. Kill the szlachta that menaces you from the shadows.

Go down into the depression and face two more szlachta, then kill them and proceed up the path. You soon encounter a szlachta feeding on a dead horse and his friend—kill the vermin!

Szlachta feeding on a horse.

Following a wooden walkway over a larger room, you soon reach an area where the passage opens up. Upon entering, you realize it is an ambush! A pack of rats surrounds you and you must fight your way out.

Battling Rats

The rats attack you on three fronts—from behind where you entered, from the other passage to your left, and from inside the large chamber itself. To avoid being surrounded, it's best to turn around and fight your way back the way you came. Once you have dispatched the rats blocking your path, you can make a stand in the narrower passageway where the rats cannot surround you!

After killing the rats, you can explore the large chamber. There are goodies to loot (coins and potions) and a couple more szlachta to kill. If you go up the ramp to the stone platform, you can see a boarded up passage. This can be opened from Level Two of the mines and is a useful short-cut should you need it later.

As you follow the passage out of the chamber, you discover the first of several rat holes. The little monsters have tunneled through much of the mines and can emerge en masse from these cracks in the wall. Normally only one rat will emerge at a time, but occasionally larger groups can come out in a feeding frenzy. Pass these holes with care. You can tell if rats are about to swarm by their loud squeaking!

After crossing several wooden platforms over bigger rooms, the path leads you into a larger chamber. Here you will meet your first szlachta boss. Tougher and fiercer than their smaller cousins, these nasties wield bones as weapons and present a greater challenge to you. As always, try to break up the group in the room, luring out the szlachta and rats before fighting the boss. Rewards await your victory, as there is a treasure chest to loot.

Soon you have to fight another szlachta boss, and then more rats. Experienced as you are by now, these fights should be much easier. As the walkway continues out over water, you reach the transition to the next level.

Level 2: Den of Evil

The veins of silver are purer in this part of the mines, giving the walls a bluish tint. Many of the caverns here are natural—carved by erosion and water—rather than made by men. The Tzimisce and their servants have begun modifying this region to suit their purposes. The lanterns are gone and have been replaced by blazing sconces carved out of the walls—their flickering flames reveal water moving in the depths. Consequently, this level is darker and wetter than the previous one.

A long, winding passage breaks out in a large natural chamber. There is a fight here, but also great treasure—you'll find the Silver Shield near an overturned mine cart! This shield should improve your chances of survival in the fights to come. Alternate between using it and the torch, depending on whether you need to see or fight.

As you follow the passage, fighting your way past the rats, you come out into a room split by a great chasm with a narrow wooden bridge spanning the abyss. If you enter the room and move toward the bridge, rats will ambush you from a hole and szlachta will close in for the kill. See if you can lure any of them away from the rest to avoid being overwhelmed.

After crossing the bridge, you'll come to a passageway that leads off to the left, which will take you back to the first level of the mines. (Should you need to return to town, take this passage and visit Anezka and Jiri!) Once you have been through this passage one way, it will be open to return you to this spot from Level One.

As you move onward, you approach the main event for this level. The narrow passages open up into a large chamber with an underground river blocking your progress.

Monsters approach as you near the water wheel.

As you take in the view, shapes shamble out of the darkness—two more szlachta!

Battling War Ghouls

The war ghoul is a dangerous opponent. Fleshcrafted by its Tzimisce masters, it is a foul thing. One arm has been bonecrafted into a wicked blade and its pestilent flesh hides powerful muscles. The beast is strong enough to impale you on its blade arm and hurl you backward. To fight it requires careful timing and a dash of luck. Pull back whenever it readies its arm so that you can dodge its powerful strike, then hit it hard to keep it off balance.

Once you have defeated your opponents, you will have to puzzle out a way to cross the water. An abandoned water wheel stands motionless—once used by the miners to keep these levels free of water. Throwing the lever brings the machine to life and the water will begin to drain away. While the water drains, go into the side chamber beyond the wheel and loot the potions and barrels.

Once the water level has fallen, a strip of dry land emerges. When you cross the river, more szlachta and a war ghoul will attack!

As the path narrows and descends into the bowels of the earth, you are forced to fight another szlachta! The path splits here, one branch leading upward to a wide plateau. There's some loot up there to help you, including two stakes.

Using Stakes

Wooden stakes make powerful weapons against vampires. Although they do little damage (only 20 as opposed to a broadsword's 30), they do possess one advantage over other weapons: Should you pierce the heart of a vampire with a stake, it will be rendered immobile for a time. The chance to do so is not great (critical hits are calculated by comparing your Dexterity and the Accuracy of the weapon to the target's defenses), but if you succeed your opponent is helpless.

Continuing onward, you enter the gateway to Ahzra's Lair. The stone here is carved into an elaborate entranceway, but only few rats guard it. Look for treasure before venturing into the darkness of Level Three.

23

Level 3: The Lair of Ahzra

This is very small level—basically, just an arena in which to fight Ahzra. The stone here is stained blood red, perhaps by ore deposits washed down from the surface, perhaps by darker things…

The antechamber where you enter has a treasure chest in a pool of stagnant water and two healing potions on a pile of crates. Equip yourself and proceed down the stairs.

A long stone staircase twists down to an open arena area. When you reach the bottom, Christof will call out the demons of the mines and Ahzra will answer.

Ahzra the Unliving

Type	Monstrous Vampire
Description	Ahzra is a Tzimisce vampire furthering her clan's conquest of Prague. She is hideously inhuman due to the use of the flesh-crafting powers of the discipline of Vicissitude and has the skin of a fallen werewolf foe wrapped about her shoulder.
Health	200
Soak	30/30/0
Damage	30 A
Powers	Ahzra can use Blood Healing, increase her strength with Blood Strength, and even summon szlachta to her side with the Beckoning.
Weaknesses	Ahzra is overconfident and will not use the full-range of her vampiric powers.
Tactics	Ahzra is a tough opponent and, unless you can weaken her fast by using any holy water or numina scrolls you have collected, it will be a very difficult fight. The best way to overcome her is to learn the pattern of her attacks, retreating as she prepares to bite and attacking her as she recovers. If you can keep her off-balance, it is possible to overwhelm her before she can kill you. Remember that healing salves take a short time to take effect, so use them in good time and pull away from her as you heal. You don't want to be using the potion just as she kills you!

After Ahzra dies you feel an almost palpable relief.

Quest Fulfilled: Reclaim the Bonn Silver Mines

New Quest : Return to St. Thomas

You can search her throne for treasure or flee immediately up the stairs. When you reach the top of the staircase, Christof will again kneel down and pick up the amulet of St. Jude. After killing Ahzra, a shortcut has opened to the surface at the top of the stairs. Take it and you will find yourself on Level One of the mines, near the entrance. Turn right and head toward the sunlight.

Interlude: Hero's return

Upon entering St. Thomas, you have a conversation with Archbishop Geza in which he will present you with the Silver Cross.

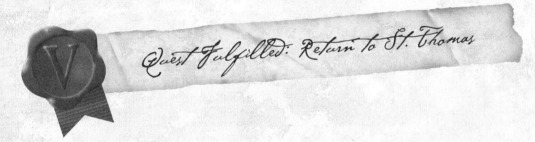

Quest Fulfilled: Return to St. Thomas

Leave the cathedral and face the adoring public, then return to the Convent to bring Anezka the good news. After talking to Anezka, you can save the game (the cross on the ledge above the beds at the far side of the infirmary allows you to do this).

Receive Quest : Protect Prague by Night

Prague By Night

The streets of Prague are haunted nightly by wandering szlachta. Explore town, killing the monsters as you find them. You may want to revisit Jiri and Unorna—Jiri may have new goods for you and Unorna will reveal more of her lore about vampires.

As you explore, notice the rats behind Jiri's (both right and left sides of smithy)—you will need them later, once you become a vampire!

When you're finished exploring, go to the clock tower (a large building where path splits right to University, and left to Jiri), and then return to the Convent. You will fight a small group of ghouls menacing a pair of ladies.

Battling Ghouls

Ghouls are mortals that have been fed vampire vitae. As such, they are stronger than mortals and can heal themselves. However, the Presmsyl ghouls are used to terrorizing civilians, not fighting armed opponents. Consequently, they present little challenge to you.

When the ghouls are dead, you hear screaming from the Convent. Go inside and slay the monsters that are threatening Anezka. Once you've defeated them, the Embrace sequence begins—sit back and watch the movie!

The Embrace

Now that you are a vampire, Ecaterina demands your submission to her will. Resist her to hold on to your humanity and she will send you and Wilhem Stryker on a quest.

Receive New Quest : Recover the Nod Fragment.
Wilhem Stryker joins coterie

Leave the University and walk downstairs to the courtyard. On the right, with University behind you, is the entrance to your haven—Wilhem will point it out to you. Enter and save the game, then spend any experience you have. As you walk the streets of Prague, Wilhem will explain vampiric existence to you. Listen carefully because he has good advice. Remember to equip Wilhem, and take him to Jiri's if you need more stuff.

Leave the old town and cross Judith Bridge, Wilhem will help you to find your first mortal victim. Feed upon the old man.

Feed on your first mortal victim.

Feeding

Feeding on the blood of mortals is necessary for vampires. Be careful not to take too much blood and kill them, as that will cost you humanity. If you are having trouble feeding (your targets keep fleeing), use Awe (the first discipline in the Presence Group) to soften them up. Any mortal under the effect of Awe will be unable to resist you and will thus be simple to feed upon.

As you leave the bridge, take the path to the left to enter Petrin Hill, then follow the path up toward the monastery. Go around the side of the monastery and enter through the large doors.

Petrin Hill Monastery

Enemies	Cappadocian vampires, zombu, skeletons, rats
Boss	Mercurio
Features	Level puzzles, pressure plate, secret room
Treasure	Femur, Nod Fragment

Overview

The Cappadocian vampires dwell in the desecrated crypts beneath the monastery. Only a few of the monks, those loyal to the master Garinol, have any idea what lurks beneath them. The Cappadocians of Prague not only follow their clan's predilection for death, but also indulge in the Cainite heresy—a blasphemous conflation of vampire myth and biblical lore. As such, the monastery is full of heretical art, *momento mori*, and the twisted products of Cappadocian research into the secrets of mortality. The monastery itself is built from beautiful white stone and the Cappadocian crypts are just as well made as the surface levels.

General Tactics

This is the first time you will face vampires as a group, and the battles here can be tricky. The same basic tactics of attempting to draw off individuals so you do not have to fight a large group apply here, only they are even more difficult. Although there are several open areas and corridors through which you must fight, many of the rooms are crowded with furniture or stone pillars, making them great ambush sites. Watch out!

The Cappadocians are not strong fighters, but they more than make up for this shortcoming with the help of their servants—the walking dead. Zombu, corpse minions, and skeletons all fight at their masters' sides and you can easily be overwhelmed by the tide of the dead.

Because the Cappadocians are often ascetics—denying themselves the blood to come closer to the secrets of the grave—they are often hungry, so beware that many will attempt to feed upon intruders, seeing your character as a way to slake their thirst. Always attempt to rescue any character that is being fed upon by another vampire—not only will they lose precious blood, but the bites of other Cainites can be deadly!

Navigating the Monastery

The monastery is clearly laid out—the Cappadocians have not designed their lair for defense. Generally, wide corridors open up into smaller shrines and laboratories. Each area is self-contained and you can progress through the underground chambers, taking each alone.

Several areas of the monastery are locked off, so you will have to find switches or keys to open these doors—make note of them so you can return quickly to where you need to be.

Monastery 1: Blasphemous Experiments

The brick walls of the lower level of the human monastery quickly pass, to be replaced by white stone adorned with the clan symbols of the Cappadocians. On this level of their lair the Gravediggers perform strange experiments, so expect to see many of the walking dead and laboratories in which these vampires perform their work.

As you enter the Petrin Hill Monastery, the human monks go about their business—they are accustomed to strange visitors at night and so make little note of your character's presence. The small reading room to the right contains some treasure, and you can feed on the hapless monks if you need more vitae.

Progressing down the corridor you soon meet the guards of the crypts—two vampires guard the door into the lower levels. Searching this small room, you can find treasure and leather armor—its protection will be most welcome soon.

Look Carefully

Always check the corners of rooms and always rotate the camera to look behind—treasure may be hidden there and it would be a shame to miss out on any of the loot! If some corners are too dark to be clearly seen, equip a torch to illuminate them.

A staircase leads further down, precariously situated over a vast pit, a statue watches you silently as you kill the lone guard and advance into the lair proper. In a large room with a huge central pillar, you meet a group of Cappadocians and the walking dead—the corpses hanging from the walls are a mute testament to your fate should you fail to destroy your enemies here.

Stairs lead out of this room into a chamber dominated by a mural of Caine's damnation—the residents will try to stop you, but you should be able to win clear over the Cappadocians here. The exits from this room are sealed by iron portcullises—a secret switch still needs to be found!

Christof and Wilhem stand in front of the mural.

If you go down the hall past the skeleton archer, you'll discover an open laboratory—bodies are dissected on slabs and some have already been animated to attack you. This is a fierce battle in crowded quarters. After killing the guards and looting the room, you will find a Scroll of Awaken—this is a powerful discipline that can stir a vampire out of torpor and is the only way to resurrect a fallen character at this point in the game. Just behind and to the side of the door is a switch that will open one of the portcullises in the mural chamber.

Battling Groups

When fighting multiple enemies, it makes sense for your entire coterie to concentrate on the most dangerous creature—in this case, the Cappadocians and not their servants. If the coterie AI is set to Neutral, the other characters in your group will follow your lead, but may attack other enemies as they see fit. To make sure everyone concentrates on one foe, use the CTRL key and left-click to make them attack one target.

The switch opens the passage into a second laboratory where several of the walking dead are newly animated by their Cappadocian mistress. After destroying these abominations, you can find a shield and the switch that will open the final portcullis, allowing you to progress down the stairs. Fight your way through another room where vampires stand ready to repel your intrusion, then a small antechamber guarded by the dead. You'll find the stairs down into the heart of the crypts. A pair of skeletons will attempt to stop you. Force your way past them and continue down to Level Two.

Battling Skeletons

Skeletons are virtually invulnerable to Lethal damage, so the best way to fight them is by using blunt or bashing weapons such as a mace. It makes sense to equip your coterie with a variety of weapons in order to inflict a range of damage types upon your foes. Another useful trick is to equip your second character (Wilhem in this case) with a torch, instead of a shield or two-handed weapon, so you can see what you're doing.

Monastery 2

This level is entirely private—no human has ever walked its halls, so the Cappadocians follow their dark worship openly. There are several shrines and chapels celebrating the Cappadocians' worship of death and Caine and the strange burial chamber where newly embraced vampires are exposed to the experience of death.

You enter Level Two by way of a large room with an ornate floor and shrines off to the side. Your enemies will attempt to overwhelm you here, but you should be able to draw them off toward the door if you move carefully. In the middle of the floor is a pile of gold—beware, it's a trap for mercenary opponents! If you touch the gold, fire will crash down the ceiling upon you. However, this trap can be used to your advantage. Grab the gold and pull back as you are attacked—there's a chance that your enemy will fall foul of the fire!

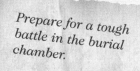

Be More Persuasive

The Brujah discipline of Presence contains the power Awe that draws a victim to your side. Wilhem has this power and Christof can develop it as an excellent way of pulling enemies from a group into your clutches. Awe is also a good way to feed upon humans, making them far more compliant to a vampire's wishes.

The double stairs exiting this chamber lead into a large room—one of the clan gathering halls. It is guarded, but since Garinol is gone, there is no meeting taking place. The next room seems out-of-place amongst the splendor of the rest of the crypts—piles of dirt and sand litter the floor and a rickety wooden plank leads up into darkness. To the left are a blocked door and a chapel full of pillars, with both vampires and the walking dead hiding in the gloom. Kill them and loot the chapel, but the door remains locked. The wooden plank seems to be the only way forward.

Climb the wooden plank into the burial room. Kill the Cappadocian on the ledge overlooking it all, and then proceed in. You will be swarmed by zombu and Cappadocians. Kill them. At the far end of the chamber is a lever that opens the doors. There is also a chest and a spiked mace to loot.

Prepare for a tough battle in the burial chamber.

Go back into the room and pass through the newly unlocked door—it opens into a narrow room with a chapel to the left and the door down to the right. Once you've killed the Cappadocian and zombu in the room, enter the chapel. If you look closely at the altar, you will see it has a secret panel. Open it and loot the gold inside. As you return to the main room, a section of the wall slowly moves out of place—you've discovered a secret room!

Two Cappadocians and the walking dead guard the secret shrine. After dispatching them, you are free to loot its treasure, including the mystical artifact Femur of an Elder Tzimisce!

Identifying Objects

Some of the objects you find—especially those with special or mystical properties—may show up as "unidentified" in the rollover text. To identify such items, you must use the Auspex discipline Spirit's Touch, which reveals the hidden history of any object. Neither Christof nor Wilhem will have developed this discipline at this point in the game; however, you may have found a scroll of Spirit's Touch as treasure. If not, then you may also buy one from Unorna.

With your new treasure, go through the door that leads to Level Three.

Monastery 3: Temple of Death

This is the heart of the Cappadocians' lair. Here you will find the rooms of both Garinol and Mercurio, and the dark temple where the clan worships.

A dark corridor with an earthen floor leads into the heart of the Cappadocian temple. As you walk down the dirt corridor, a Cappadocian will rise up. Fight your way through to the main room on the level, passing Mercurio's study guarded by a skeleton.

As you work your way forward, you will pass a side corridor filled with dirt. Enter it and kill the vampires that rise from their sleep, then approach the door at its end. It is locked, so you will have to search further for the key.

At the end of long corridor, a pressure pad at the side of the floor opens the portcullis up the stairs. However, once one character has entered the room at the top, the door will shut behind him! You must fight alone.

After the Cappadocians and their servants have been dispatched, your second character will be able to enter the room. Fight your way up the double stairs until you stand in front of the bone mural. The key to Garinol's study is resting in a stone plinth beneath the decorated walls.

Lobster Pot Rooms

This is the first of several rooms in the game in which the door closes behind one or more characters, trapping them in a fight to the death. The principle behind such rooms is that your enemies seal the door as you enter to destroy you more easily and that one of them has the key. Killing the enemy that has the token key will unlock the door, allowing you to leave again.

Use the bone key to enter Garinol's study, then fight the Cappadocian and her pet zombu!

On Garinol's desk (the room at the end of the walkway), you can find treasure and the Lamia Skull. Don't forget to loot the treasure chest! Down the stairs to either side of Garinol's room is his library—two Cappadocians guard his books and some minor loot.

Go back outside and proceed toward the exit, then stop at the door that was locked earlier, guarded by a skeleton. With the Lamia Skull, you can unlock the mystical bonds on the door and enter Mercurio's study!

Mercurio will attempt to convince you to join him and turn on your friend, Wilhem. Should you consider such a despicable choice, you will lose humanity. Fight Mercurio and bring his scheming to an end!

Mercurio, Childe of Garinol

Type	Ambitious Vampire Necromancer
Description	Appearing as a humble monk, these humble trappings hide a rotten heart. Mercurio is unpreposing, except for the gleam of madness and ambition in his eyes.
Health	300
Soak	0/0/0
Damage	75 B
Powers	Cappadocian clan disciplines at level 3 (Common, Auspex, Mortis, Fortitude)
Weaknesses	Mercurio wears no armor, and this gives you a chance. Hit him hard with the best weapons you have and lure him into physical conflict.
Tactics	Make sure that Christof and Wilhem are attacking from opposite sides. If they are too close together, Mercurio can strike them both with Plague Wind or Black Death.

Once Mercurio is dead, he drops the Nod Fragment that he was guarding so fiercely—pick it up. You can search the room and find his journal, as well as treasure to loot. Congratulations! Reading these documents will uncover the secret of Mercurio's plot: He sought to use the Golem for his own ends!

The Golem of Prague

The Golem of Prague is actually a famous story/legend. Look for it in books of folklore and imagine you are taking part in events that will be remembered a thousand years later!

Reading Documents

Right-click on any document in your inventory to read it. This will pause the game and bring up a text box on screen while the document is read. You can find many letters, journals, and fragments of ancient knowledge scattered throughout the game. Read them all for a deeper understanding of what's going on.

You are now free to leave the monastery. Walk through the deserted halls to the exit. If you're low on blood, you can feed from the monks on the upper level. Once you leave the monastery, Wilhem keeps his promise and takes you to see Anezka. After this sad meeting you will find yourself on the streets of Prague behind the Convent.

As you return to the University to deliver the Nod Fragment to Ecaterina, you may encounter the crazed vampire, Libussa, on the streets. She makes little sense at this point, but later you will realize that she is one of the servants of Vukodlak, the Voivode!

Upon returning to the University, Ecaterina is delighted with your success. She wants to use the information you have gathered for political ends. Should you fail to protest the morality of her choices, you will lose humanity. Whatever choice you make, she will send you to the Jewish Ghetto, the North Quarter of Prague, to carry information to the rabbi.

Medieval Ghettos

The Medieval period was a time of great racism. In many cities of Europe, the Jewish population was restricted to a certain area called a ghetto and suffered under many unfair laws relating to trade and curfew. Christof is very enlightened in that he treats Jews as human beings with full rights and sees his moral obligation toward them.

Quest Fulfilled: Recover the Nod Fragment
New Quest : Kill the Golem

Leave the University and proceed toward the Clock Tower—the door to the North Quarter is just beyond the Tower. Before you go, you may want to visit your haven to save the game and spend the Experience Points you have earned. Remember that Wilhem will have earned experience too, so do not neglect him.

PRAGUE
(north quarter)

Enemies	Maqqabah the Golem

This night in the Jewish Quarter everyone is afraid: The Golem that the Rabbi created to protect them has run amok, destroying buildings outside the Synagogue. Follow the narrow streets past locked buildings and shuttered windows until you encounter Mendel, the rabbi's son. He will tell you that his father is dead and no one has the power to stop the rampaging Golem and retrieve its Shem—the mystical power that keeps it animate.

Go through the tunnel near Mendel and enter the courtyard opposite the Synagogue. The Golem has been wrecking this area of the North Quarter and several buildings have already been reduced to rubble.

Hit and run, and especially run if Maqqabah lifts his hands above his head (the preparation for his smash attack). Mental powers are very effective against the simple-witted beast, so use Awe to keep it confused and unable to focus its attacks upon you. Given that Maqqabah is a simple creature, it is possible that its attention will become focused on a single member of your coterie. If this becomes the case, a new tactic becomes available to you. Take control of the character the golem is focusing on, then run away making sure you are always close, but out of attack range of Maqqabah. The golem will continue to chase that one character, allowing the second member of your coterie to attack him from behind!

Once you have destroyed the Golem, its Shem will drop to the floor. You must take this to Mendel to prevent its power from being abused ever again. You can also see a wooden door that leads out of this courtyard. This is the entrance to the graveyard and you will be returning here soon, so remember the route!

Take the Shem to Mendel. He will suggest that you take it Garinol, the leader of the Cappadocians.

New Quest : Bring the Shem to Garinol

Leave the North Quarter and, from the Old Town, cross the Judith Bridge and ascend Petrin Hill. Garinol and his childe, Serena, are waiting for you. Despite any fear you might have, Garinol harbors no animosity for you—he grants leave that Serena might travel with you!

New Coterie Member: Serena
Quest Fulfilled: Bring the Shem to Garinol

You now have no immediate directions from your sire, and no clues as to where you should go. Leave the monastery and go into Golden Lane. Visit Unorna—she has news of Anezka for you—then return to your haven to rest. Serena will try to comfort you.

When you wake the next night (time passes while you rest/spend experience in your haven; it is one of the few measures of time vampires who dwell in eternal night have). Ecaterina summons you before her. She also has news of Anezka, but more urgently, she has demands to make of the Prince of Prague, Rudolph Brandl.

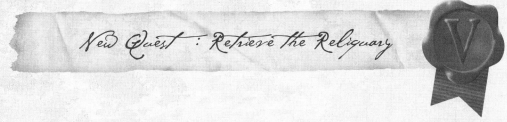

Vampire Titles

Vampires are creatures of great tradition and one of these is that the eldest amongst the broods in any city shall be Prince and have domin-ion over the others. Prince Brandl is a weak example of his kind, but his skill at political maneuvering keeps the throne under his control. During the story you see him using the Brujah clan to contain the power of the Tremere while remaining neutral in person. A clever vampire is Brandl!

You and your coterie are taken to the Prince's chambers, along with Ecaterina and Cosmas. Your sire makes demands of the Prince, who agrees to hear her petition only if she retrieves a great holy relic for him.

New Quest : Retrieve the Reliquary

Once the audience is finished, leave Prince Brandl's chambers, down the stairs, and go through the courtyard of Prague castle. The exit to Judith Bridge is on the opposite side of the courtyard, past the statue of the mounted warrior.

The relic you seek is kept within the Cathedral crypts, inaccessible to vampires because of the power of Faith that protects the building. The only way to gain entry is to use the secret tunnels beneath the foundations of the building inhabited by the Nosferatu. The leader of this clan, Josef, makes his haven in the graveyard beyond the North Quarter. Return to where you fought the Golem and proceed through the wooden doors. The statue of a weeping mother dominates the ancient graveyard; behind this lies a narrow path into a burial chamber where Josef lurks.

Josef is willing to let you gain access to his underground domain, but first he demands you bring the vitae of a beautiful elder, Cainite. Only Ecaterina fulfils this demand, so you must return to your sire and ask for her blood.

New Quest : Bring Beautiful Elder Vitae to Josef

Ecaterina can be found in the University and is happy to grant you a chalice of her blood. Take this to Josef and he will open the gate into the tunnels for you. However, he will warn you that he has no control over the inhabitants of the Tunnels. They respect his power, but will not willingly allow strangers to enter there.

Quest Fulfilled: Bring beautiful elder vitae to Josef

Josef's Tunnels

Enemies	Rats, Ghouls, Nosferatu
Bosses	Nosferatu boss, Vaclav
Features	Invisible enemies, some levers
Treasure	Reliquary, bastard sword, Gangrel Eye, Tome of Animalism

Overview

The Nosferatu tunnels present a mix of the history of the city—forgotten storerooms, ancient Roman sewers, the foundation of the great city buildings, and deep tunnels carved by the undead. The Nosferatu are great hoarders and gleaners, and treasures and trash lie scattered throughout their domain—you can find rags treated with as much ceremony as precious stones in this underground bedlam.

General Tactics

The greatest danger you face in the tunnels is that the Nosferatu have the power to render themselves invisible. This Obfuscate Discipline makes them deadly in combat because they can attack from any direction and slip away before you can counterattack. The Nosferatu will appear for a moment as they attack—this is your best chance to target them. You can also use your coterie's disciplines to detect them. The powers of Heightened Senses and Eyes of the Beast can see through the deception. Serena will have Heightened Senses and she is invaluable to you in the tunnels.

The stronger Nosferatu have weapons and their leaders wear black cassocks, mocking the priests who damn their kind. Try to destroy these enemies first as they are the most dangerous in combat.

There is much treasure to be found among the Nosferatu hoards. Search everywhere for items buried with the dead or dragged from the surface into the tunnels. Unless you want to make several trips back to the surface to sell the items you find, it pays to be selective in what you choose to carry with you.

Navigating the Tunnels

In several places the tunnels loop back on themselves and, unless you're paying attention, you may get turned around. The easiest landmarks to orient yourself around are the coffins of the dead and treasure chests (if they are open, you have already searched the area).

As you progress onward, the appearance of your surroundings change: Earth gives way to stone, stone to sewer channels, and these to caverns. Make note of these changes so even if you do get lost, you can orient yourself easily.

Josef's Tunnels 1: Realm of the Dead

The coffins of the dead in these earthen tunnels have been violated and lie scattered about. The early sections of the level are directly under the graveyard, should you choose you could disturb the rest of the dead to loot their burial trinkets. Here and there the stone walls of foundations and crypts lie exposed and tunnels wind their way past antique sewers and modern cellars.

From the crypt entrance, you come into low earthen tunnels, tree roots break through the ceiling and the bones of the deceased can be seen entwined amongst them. Two of the Nosferatu immediately oppose, shifting in and out of sight as they attack. The tunnel winds off in two directions—Both meet later in the level, so take whichever one seems most inviting. Along each branch you find coffins and Nosferatu lurking in the shadows. As you round each bend, expect more Nosferatu to oppose you. Do not try running away into areas you have not yet explored, because even more enemies always await. The Nosferatu will use their servants to set up ambushes, luring you toward the visible foes while they wait, invisible and ready to summon vermin to fight you.

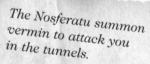

The Nosferatu summon vermin to attack you in the tunnels.

Battling Summoned Creatures

Many vampires can summon other creatures to fight with them—ranging from the mundane, such as rats, up to wraiths and elementals. In general, it is best to ignore the summoned creature as it has only a temporary existence. Instead, concentrate on the vampiric master who can, in any case, summon more creatures. Later in the game you will be able to summon your own allies.

Once the two branches have met again, follow the single passage along the stone wall. It soon opens up into the abandoned catacombs of the church. Check the corners and ledges for any abandoned grave goods. As the passage turns sharply left, you see a lever set in the floor.

Pulling it slides back a section of wall behind you. The hidden room is guarded as it contains treasure and has a trap. As you walk in, a hidden trigger disgorges burning oil from the walls—be careful or you'll be scorched! Leaving this room, you follow a long stone corridor. Ahead of you down small steps wait more of the Lepers. If you charge them, their ghoul servants will attack you from out of sight, around the corner. Be careful here and draw as many enemies as you can back into the corridor.

Moving deeper, you descend stairs and reach a passage barred by a portcullis. To the side, under the stairs, is a chamber containing a lever. Defeat the guards and throw the switch to open the portcullis, then keep moving. Through the portcullis is a long room alongside a water channel. Several Nosferatu are gathered here and they will attack as soon as you enter. At the end of the chamber are dark rooms with more enemies and a narrow staircase that leads upward.

Climb the staircase and you'll find yourself in a series of cellars and storerooms—the Nosferatu have been stealing from the inhabitants of Prague. The rooms are all guarded, but a careful search will reveal gold and other treasures. Through a broken wall, the cellars give way to part of the sewer system where a strong group of Nosferatu swarm you.

Battling Against Ambushes

Your coterie is at a disadvantage as it comes through the narrow break in the wall and down into the sewers. Whoever goes first will be attacked viciously with no time to ready a defense. It is possible to use vampiric disciplines to circumvent this problem—Wilhem or Christof can use Celerity to sprint past the choke zone. Using thrown weapons to clear a space as you enter is also a useful option: Holy Water or Greek Fire will scatter the defenders.

You enter another storeroom through the next broken wall. After fighting, you can progress through the shattered wall to the next level.

Josef's Tunnels 2: Sewer System

This deeper level of the tunnels is dank and dark. Depressions have filled with water to become small pools and stalagmites and stalactites are common. The vast stone foundations of Prague's ancient buildings show as great stone walls, in some places precariously shored up where the tunneling has weakened them. Late in the level you enter a by-way of the city's old sewer system and finally the portal to the labyrinth where no human being has ever set foot.

The path here winds around the vast foundations of the cathedral. In dark corners and by pools of stagnant water the Nosferatu lurk ready to preserve their solitude. You will have to fight you way through each corner and twist and turn of the passage. As the passage moves between the stone walls of the foundations an odd piece of stonework catches your eyes: There is a secret room here! To open it Use Heightened Senses (Auspex first power).

The room is a forgotten chapel to some ancient vampire or lost god. Inside is a Tome of Animalism (discipline tomes can teach you new powers of the blood) and the Gangrel Eye, a long lost mystical relic. The Eye will allow you to see the hidden Nosferatu, making your task much easier.

Beyond the secret shrine the passage splits, leading in separate directions around the ancient stonework. The two forks meet up again, so take either path and watch out for the guards. The Nosferatu will continue to oppose you, rising from the stagnant pools to kill all intruders. There are several such points where the vampires will come at you. Advance carefully so two groups do not attack you at once.

At the end of the twisting pathways is a staircase carved into the rock. Climb it and be prepared for battle. At the top, the area opens up into sandstone passages, the antique sewers beneath the Cathedral itself. As you enter the sandstone passages, be prepared for a really tough fight. There are several Nosferatu and their boss wields an axe.

Battling the Nosferatu Leader

Expect a great deal of brutality here. The Nosferatu leader is powerful and dangerous and you are not fighting him alone. He will not hesitate to feed upon your coterie, hurting them and draining precious blood with great speed. Make sure that Christof is carrying the Gangrel Eye so he can see this foe and concentrate your attacks upon him. It would be a good idea to activate your disciplines before you enter the sewer so that effects such as Potence and Celerity are ready when the fight begins. Ensure that your coterie has plenty of blood—they'll need it.

Just around the corner from the ambush site is a staircase, which leads up to the Golden Lane. This gives you a chance to sell the loot you have collected and, if necessary, feed upon the towns-folk to revive your coterie. Once you're ready, return through the Golden Lane entrance and proceed down the last turn of the passage.

At the very end of the level a friendly Nosferatu, Illig, guards the door to the labyrinth. After you have talked to him and received the clue to the Labyrinth, move through the door into Level Three.

Josef's Tunnels 3: The Labyrinth

This level opens with the Labyrinth. A product of the master architect Zelios, it is used as a place of meditation by the Nosferatu who seek to understand their damned condition. Beyond the Labyrinth are the crypts of the Cathedral with their stone sarcophagi and urns for the dead. The final crypt is that of King Vaclav, a vengeful wraith. You must kill him to claim the reliquary.

The Labyrinth is a beautiful sequence of staircases and carved pillars. Each staircase splits into two, leading to separate doors, and on each pillar is carved an episode from Caine's life. To pass through the Labyrinth you must read from each pillar, and then take the door that seems most appropriate based on the inscription.

The sequence you must follows chronological events in Caine's life. Each door is marked with an icon depicting a moment in Cainite history. The order is as follows:

1. Caine (red face)

2. City of Enoch (castle walls)

3. The Second Generation (three faces)

4. The Great Deluge (water waves)

5. The Thirteen Clans (13 ankhs)

Beyond the Labyrinth are the crypts of the Cathedral. As you move past the tombs of the great of Prague, Nosferatu and rats will attack you. You should be ready for them at this point. In a large room ringed by the dead, iron bars block your way. After you have dispatched the room's guardians, you can throw a lever to raise the bars. Be careful when searching the room—engravings in the floor have been enchanted to deter trespassers by blasting fire from the ceiling should you fail to move carefully.

Before you go up the stairs, pay attention to the wall by the second lever. There is a pressure pad that opens a niche in the wall further up. Hurry up the stairs and in an alcove guarded by two Nosferatu you find a bastard sword—a most efficient weapon! Continue climbing the stairs and enter the next level of the crypt.

Here stone sarcophagi are lined up against the walls. Search behind them and you'll find treasures that the Nosferatu have stolen from the dead. There is little opposition here as an aura of gloom keep even the Nosferatu away. Walk carefully forward and the crypts open up into a large room with a tomb and altar. A shadow figure floats before the tomb—the wraith of King Vaclav!

The Wraith of King Vaclav floats before you.

43

The Wraith of King Vaclav

Type	Insane spirit of the Dead
Description	A translucent, twisted figure that rises from the tomb to oppose you.
Health	200
Soak	Immune/60/60; Immune to Cold and Electricity
Damage	65 Cold
Powers	Vaclav carries with him the aura of death. He can drain your life-force (blood) and suck life (health) from you with a touch. He may also Call Lightning, Mesmerize, Heightened Senses, Heal, Strength, and use Theft of Vitae.
Weaknesses	Vaclav is bound to his tomb, so he cannot follow you. That means if things go badly, you can always just run!
Tactics	Back away, using any ranged attacks or disciplines to disable him. Vaclav is immune to mortal weapons, so this can be a very difficult fight. Vaclav is the first spirit you encounter on your journey. Spirits make dangerous opponents because they are immaterial and, hence, invulnerable to physical attacks. The only sure way to damage spirits is with Aggravated damage (such as that caused by Feral Claws) or by Elemental damage (fire, holy water, etc.) Whenever you fight a spirit, make sure you have attacks that can harm them. Coterie members without such attacks should be pulled out of combat, or set to use mental powers that can distract the foe.

Battling Spirits

Vaclav is the first spirit you encounter on your journey. Spirits make dangerous opponents because they are immaterial and, hence, invulnerable to physical attacks. The only way to damage spirits is with Aggravated damage (such as that caused by Feral Claws) or by Elemental damage (fire, holy water, etc.). Whenever you fight a spirit, make sure you have attacks that can harm them. Coterie members without such attacks should be pulled out of combat, or set to use mental powers that can distract the foe.

After Vaclav has been banished back to his tomb (you cannot kill the true dead), you'll be able to open the door that leads out of his tomb. Climb the stairs and push open the fake stone wall to enter the resting-place of the Reliquary. Here you will find some treasure and the Reliquary itself. Pick it up carefully, and then return through the crypts to the Labyrinth.

Leaving the Labyrinth is easier than entering it. As soon as you've left the crypts and enter the Labyrinth, go through the large wooden door. This will take you back to where Illig waits, near the shortcut up to the Golden Lane. Finally, leave the tunnels and breathe the fresh air under a night sky.

From Golden Lane, you should return to Prince Brandl's chambers. Follow the path you took from his chambers in reverse and you will find yourself before his throne where you can give the Reliquary to him.

Quest Fulfilled: Retrieve Reliquary

Upon completing your quest, Prince Brandl will listen to your and Ecaterina's request to attack the Tremere Chantry and free the slaves with more favor. If you do not speak up to oppose the prince's amorality, you will lose humanity; however, should you anger the Prince, he will express his displeasure in no uncertain terms.

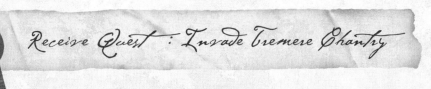

Receive Quest : Invade Tremere Chantry

The Tremere Chantry is hidden at the top of Golden Lane. Before you go there, you should visit your haven to rest and spend experience, as well as visiting both Unorna and Jiri to sell loot and buy any new gear you need. When you're ready, proceed up Golden Lane and enter the 'pharmacy' now exposed as the Tremere Chantry

Ardan's Chantry

Enemies	Tremere, hoppers, elementals, a gargoyle
Boss	Ardan of Golden Lane
Features	Hermetic Circles
Treasure	Ivory Bow, Sire's Finger, much loot
New PC	Erik

Overview

Hidden behind a humble pharmacy on Golden Lane, the Tremere Chantry in Prague is an outpost for the clan. Besieged by the hostile local Cainites, especially those of Clan Tzimisce, the Tremere have adopted a siege mentality. Under the guidance of their leader, Ardan, they have been tapping into the magical potential of the land to grow a great mystical tree that will enhance their magic powers. The rooms of the Chantry reflect their occupants' obsession with magic—mystical glyphs line the walls, light is provided by strange bale-fires, and magic circles can be found in every room. As a studious clan descended from mortal wizards, there are many libraries and workstations for their mystical experiments.

General Tactics

The Tremere are dangerous foes who combine disciplines that control the mind with those that command the elements. Expect to be confused and controlled by the evil wizards, as well as burned by fire and struck by lightning. Luckily, these powers have a high cost in blood and the Tremere will soon exhaust their reserves. Once they begin to run low on blood, you'll discover that they are weak in hand-to-combat, allowing you to overwhelm them with relative ease.

Fortunately, the elemental forces that the Tremere call upon cannot distinguish between friend and foe. Try to make sure that some of your foes' line-of-sight is blocked by their comrades and you may be lucky enough to provoke them into striking each other.

Within the magically charged Chantry, the Tremere have one more dangerous power—translocation. By concentrating on the flow of magic from the great tree, they can move from place to place to stay out of your weapons' range. Be ready for this and strike them when they're close to you.

To make up for their physical limitations, the Tremere create alchemical servants such as hoppers. Beware of these little beasts—they can swarm you and easily bring down one of your coterie members.

46

Navigating the Chantry

The Tremere love efficiency, so the Chantry follows a fairly simple design of large rooms connected by wide corridors. The branches and roots of the Great Tree connect all the levels with stairways following the trunk down.

Ardan's Chantry 1: Branches of the Tree

Starting in a humble shop, this level follows the upper branches down into the Tremere Chantry. This level is composed primarily of the studies and libraries of the resident Tremere, where they work to combine hermetic alchemy with the power of the blood.

Go through the shop and into the backroom, then pull aside the curtain. Behind it, stairs wind their way down around the trunk of a giant tree. Bale-fire glows from its branches as you descend deep into the earth.

The first room you enter is a small one containing a magic circle and your first swarm of hoppers. The little beasts have a voracious appetite for blood, so dispatch them quickly.

Magic Circles

Drawing on the power of the land and their enchanted tree, the Tremere have created many hermetic circles throughout the Chantry. Marked with arcane symbols and burning with unholy fire, these circles pierce the walls separating this world from the spirit realm and have strange effects. If you draw too close to a circle, it will activate and bring something from the other side—sometimes strange bloodstones, more often hoppers, or even elementals. You must choose carefully whether to approach the circles or not.

The larger room beyond this small one contains Tremere at work and more hoppers. Try to position yourself so the Tremere will hurl fire at their comrades and servants instead of at your coterie. Carefully loot the room—you can find many supplies the Tremere use in their studies, like scrolls, precious stones, and vitae. On a plinth in the corner lies a valuable artifact—The Sire's Finger.

Another similar workroom lies beyond this room with more Tremere to oppose you. Here the passage forks into two. The left fork leads into a small library and a room with many Tremere studying the mystic tomes. Be prepared for a tough fight as you dispatch the wizards and claim their treasure for yourself.

The right fork takes you into another laboratory where the warlocks have summoned many hoppers. Two doorways lead out of this room. The lower of the two doors opens into another study with a larger hermetic circle in an alcove. Resting here is the Ivory Bow, a powerful Cainite weapon that the Tremere are studying.

To use a missile weapon, simply equip one of your characters with it (it takes both weapon and shield slots in your inventory). If the character is AI controlled, they will use the weapon until its ammunition is exhausted, and then reload (if they have more ammunition in their inventory) or switch to a melee weapon. Because of Serena's low physical attributes, it would sensible to equip her with the bow so she does not rush into combat. Remember to keep her supplied with arrows if you do so!

Return to the laboratory and take the other door. You'll see a dark tunnel flanked by tree roots that takes you down to Level Two. If you first follow the stairs above this tunnel, you will confront more Tremere in one last study.

Ardan's Chantry 2: Trunk of the Tree

This level is for the more important Tremere to study. With larger rooms and elaborately embroidered rugs, the architectural style is more eastern, showing a Moorish influence. There are several communal Hermetic Circles where the warlocks stand safely on a platform above the circle when they perform their incantations. At the center of this level are the holding cells where slaves are kept before being sent to Vienna.

The stairs take you down past the tree and end in a pool of water, then open into one of the Tremere's sanctums. The room is richer than the communal laboratories and studies upstairs, and the Tremere will fight fiercely to defend them.

The exit from the room leads out onto a platform over a Hermetic Circle where several Tremere are performing their magic. Fight your way past them and the hoppers they have already summoned, then go through the Moorish archway. Fight your way down from the ledge and into the center of the room to release the slaves. The nun will tell you that Anezka has already been sent on to Vienna. This is confirmed by the discovery of Ardan's Manifest, the list of his slave shipments, on a nearby desk. Swear vengeance on the warlocks, then go through the arch and down the stairs.

More Tremere are working their rituals over a magic circle here. Kill them all and either go down past the circle or through the adjacent empty storeroom. Both ways lead you into a room full of Tremere who are mobilizing to stop you. Fight your way past them and descend down the stairs to Level Three.

Ardan's Chantry 3: The Roots of the Tree

This level is a single large chamber built around the roots of the Great Tree. Here the Tremere tap into the power of the earth to create their gargoyle servants, so you will face strong opposition. The roots of the tree and pillars dominate the chamber, to which the warlocks chain captives about to undergo the transformation into gargoyles. The scene is brightly lit with many bale-fires in sconces and magic circles.

You find yourself on a platform overlooking a vast chamber. Below you are Tremere, hoppers, and a captive vampire (Erik) chained to the roots of the Great Tree. Rush down the stairs and confront the evil wizards. As you approach the captive, he begs for aid. After you have dispatched the wizards and their gargoyle servant, you can free Erik from his bonds.

Erik joins the coterie

Explore the chamber, searching for treasure, and then go down the stairs at the far side, dispatching any hoppers that try to stop you.

Ardan's Chantry 4: Ardan's Sanctum

This single room is Ardan's sanctum. The warlock will try to oppose you, but you should face little difficulty in exacting vengeance upon him. Ardan will try to convince you to spare him. Do not listen and crush the slave-trading wizard!

Historical Mystery

Although it appears that you have killed Ardan, a vampire named Ardan is known to lead the Prague Chantry at least until the Nineteenth Century. Perhaps this was an impostor you faced, perhaps Ardan had some secret magic preventing his destruction, or perhaps the Tremere erased records of your attack on the Chantry from their histories and set up another vampire who has taken Ardan's name as the leader here. We may never know…

Quest Fulfilled: Invade Tremere Chantry

After destroying the Tremere Chantry, you return to Ecaterina with your news. She seeks to prevent you from seeking out Anezka, asking you what mortals matter to an immortal? Should you accept her argument, you will lose humanity, as another fragment of your mortal love slips away. Whether you defy her or not, your course is clear—you must go to Vienna, following the slave route!

Exit through the East gate of Prague and transition to Vienna.

Vienna

Vienna is an ancient and prosperous city, the center of learning and political power for this region of Eastern Europe. Less a medieval city and more of a city stumbling into the Renaissance, the streets are wider and better set out than Prague's. The Outer Stradt is a large ring-shaped street with exits at the cardinal directions to the Northern, Southern, Eastern and Western Strasse, and doors leading inward to the Inner Stradt. To reach anywhere in Vienna, you must merely follow the Outer Stradt until you reach the correct door.

The Northern Strasse, where your coterie begins, is an abandoned city gate next to a ruined church—here you make your haven. The Eastern Strasse is a bohemian district of town where you can find the Green Frog Inn and the Order of Hermes magic shop. The Southern Strasse leads to the fortress of the Tremere—the Haus de Hexe. Near this gateway is the shop of one of Vienna's finest weapon-smiths. Finally, the mansion of the slave master Orsi dominates the Western Strasse. Heavily armed knights guard each gate, keeping the peace.

The snow is falling as you enter Vienna through its abandoned north gate. The seasons have turned to winter in your travels from Prague to Vienna in search of Anezka. Go into the desecrated church on your right. Throwing the lever on the wall will open the crypt where your haven is.

When you are finished in your haven, leave the church and go into Vienna itself. Double doors open into the outer Stradt and, from here, you can explore the city. At this point, most doors are barred to you: Orsi's mansion is inaccessible, the Haus de Hexe is protected by mystical sigils, and the Teutonic Knights' headquarters is locked tight. There is a weapons shop by the entrance to the Southern Strasse, which sells finer goods than Jiri could produce.

Work your way around to the Eastern Strasse (turn left immediately after entering Outer Stradt). To your left, beyond the well, is the Order of Hermes' magic shop. Go inside, talk to Orvus, and buy any mystical items you might need. Orvus is a member of the house of mortal mages that gave rise to the Tremere. Luckily, he is more sympathetic to your cause than to his vampire cousins. Opposite the shop is a large green building—the Green Frog Inn.

At the inn, three vampires are tormenting a drunk. After talking to them, you discover they are Orsi's children—the triplets, Kazi, Teta, and Zil—and they give you an invitation to Orsi's mansion.

New Quest: Attend Count Orsi's Party

Leave the inn and walk back onto the outer Stradt. If you take the door directly in front of you, which leads into the inner Stradt, you'll follow a shortcut to Orsi's. Go straight through the Inner Stradt, marveling at the huge, gothic buildings, then take the western exit. This brings you into the Outer Stradt again, directly opposite the entrance to the mansion. Go through the door to Orsi's courtyard, and then up the sweeping marble staircase into Orsi's mansion.

Orsi has done well for himself from the profits of the slave trade. His mansion is beautiful with a polished marble floor, paintings, rich drapes, and expensive furniture. Important burghers of Vienna attend his gatherings with little idea of what their host truly is. Talk to the triplets and Orsi will come out to confront you. He withholds the information you need, instead offering you a deal: Kill his enemy, Luther Black, and he will tell you all.

Inside Orsi's mansion

Quest Fulfilled: Attend Count Orsi's Party
Receive Quest: Find Secret Entrance to Clock
Receive Quest: Kill Luther Black

The Lasombra, Luther Black's haven, is protected by the power of Faith. He has burrowed his way beneath the churches of Vienna and believes he's immune to Cainite attack. The only way to enter his demesne is to sneak in through a secret entrance inside the Astrological Clock. To get there, return to the Inner Stradt and follow the buildings to your left—looking up you can see the clock outlined against the night sky. One of the buildings is open—you can enter and climb to its upper levels, eventually emerging onto the rooftops through a window. Follow a precarious path along the rooftops until you reach the face of the clock itself. A hidden door reveals itself and takes you inside the workings of the clock!

Quest Fulfilled: Find Secret Entrance to Clock

Stephansdom

Enemies	Rats, Lasombra Ghouls, Dark Hunters
Boss	Luther Black (no fight)
Features	Avoiding sunlight and several button puzzles, our hero faces a moral choice.
Treasure	Heart Shield, Concoction, some jewelry, precious stones

Overview

The start of this level is inside the clock itself. With its complicated machinery and moving gears, it presents a puzzle in itself. Beyond the clock are colonnades between fine buildings awash with sunlight, a dangerous place for a vampire to be. As you penetrate Stephansdom itself, the lower levels are plain tunnels shored up by wooden pilings and dark storage rooms. When you finally enter Black's haven, you find rich rooms influenced by Moorish architecture leading to Luther's own resting-place—in a chapel upon a cross of purest silver!

General Tactics

The early parts of this level are difficult only because of the sunlight, which will destroy your coterie in seconds. The easiest way to move through the level is to separate your coterie (click on the green light next to the character portrait to remove them from the group). Once everyone is separated, move Christof alone through the sunlit areas. Fighting the enemies will be harder alone, but it's easy for one of your allies to move into the sunlight and perish.

The lighting on this level is not mood lighting—you can see the sunlight, and now that you're a vampire you must avoid any direct exposure to the sun's rays! In some areas it is unavoidable; the best way to get through these sections is to use Celerity so that you move faster, and Fortitude so that you have some measure of resistance to Aggravated damage.

Because it is daylight you won't face any vampires on this level, only the servants of the Lasombra. Although strong, the ghouls should prove no match for you, but the Lasombra can also summon shadows—Dark Hunters—to guard their havens. These entities are vicious fighters, resisting most forms of damage. Use Fire or Aggravated damage to harm them.

Navigating Stephansdom

The direct path through Stephansdom is very simple, but it pays to explore to find the treasures hidden throughout the level. As a general rule, moving upward leads you toward Luther's resting place, but side explorations will greatly reward you.

Stephansdom 1: The Clock Tower

You and your coterie wait for dawn to come and the gears of the clock to uncover the path. Proceed down the wooden stairs inside the clock tower, fighting your way past the two ghouls who have been sent to make sure that the tower is secure.

Elimate the ghouls on your way down the clock tower.

The walkway inside the clock has been deliberately broken, forcing you outside into the sunlit colonnades.

Sunlight and Vampires

Sunlight is anathema to vampires; the direct rays of the sun will quickly reduce even a powerful Cainite to dust. You must avoid it at all costs. Even waking and moving during the day is hard for vampires, and functioning during the daylight hours saps their strength. This explains why Orsi's knights can overwhelm you at the end of this level—the constant exposure to daylight has weakened your coterie too greatly for them to be able to resist.

Walk carefully on the shadowed side of the wall, avoiding direct sunlight. Stay in the shadows as you follow the alleyway around, fighting off attacks by ghouls and rats. Remember not to chase your enemies into the sunlight—this is what they want you to do! The alleyway bends back into the clock tower.

A swinging pendulum blocks your path. Before sneaking past it, go down the rickety wooden stairs to the basement of the clock tower. A swarm of rats guards valuable treasure, including a precious Tome of Dominate. Go back up the stairs, and then use Celerity to sprint past the pendulum—it's heavy enough to crush you should it make contact. Push the pressure pad on the wall to stop the pendulum.

Beyond this deadly trap, the alley splits into two. If you bear left, you come upon more ghouls guarding a claymore and stairs that lead down into a dark basement. A group of ghouls will oppose you here, but you're in no danger from the sun. If you turned left, the alley leads to the same cave entrance, but with fewer ghoul opponents and more danger from sunlight.

A sloping path in direct sunlight leads up to a barricaded cave. A ghoul will try to fight you in the sunlight—use your powers to lure him into the shadows.

A set of three levers is by the barricaded cave. Pull the middle one first, then the one on the right, and finally the left lever. The barricade will slide out of the way, allowing you into the cave and on to Level Two.

Stephansdom 2: Hidden Tunnels

Underground tunnels connect the secret clock entrance to the lower levels of Black's haven. You move from dark tunnels shored up by wooden pilings into the basement of Luther's manse.

Together or Apart?

Now that you're in the dark, you may reunite the coterie. Hit the Regroup button to bring everyone together and follow your lead. Consider, however, that some parts of the tunnels emerge into sunlight, so you might also decide to keep everyone separated for a while.

Moving through the tunnel, ghouls armed with crossbows attack you, then you break out into a large chamber with a swarm of rats. The ghouls are as vain as their Lasombra masters, so check the corners carefully for the precious tomes and jewelry they keep stashed. Continue to fight through the tunnel until you see sunlight again.

The alley between the buildings splits. If you go down between the buildings into sunlight, you'll fight a ghoul and some rats, and claim your loot. Proceeding upward through sunlight, you must fight the ghoul guards and then throw open the double doors that take into the basement of Stephansdom itself. The building is made of white stone with subtle engraving in the classical style. The dark basement rooms are a relief after the sunlight outside, but more ghouls oppose you.

Fight your way past the guards until stone stanchions bar further progress. If you look above the fireplace in the room, you'll see five buttons amongst the carvings. Turn around and look in the mirror on the opposite wall—two of the buttons are illuminated. Press those buttons and the stanchions will slide back into the wall! (From the left to right, the two buttons are the second and the last.)

Kill the lone ghoul blocking your way out of the basement, then head through the door.

Stephansdom 3: The Haven of Luther Black

The body of Luther's haven is made up of narrow, dark rooms with wooden floors, barely lit by candles. Dark leaded glass windows block the sunlight, and portraits of Luther and his clan stare down from the walls in the large chambers.

Reunite the coterie again and fight your way through the cellar until you come to the stairs. Follow them up, fighting ghouls at each new level. As you move higher and nearer to the roof, the wall begins to slant at an angle making the chambers claustrophobic.

When the stairs end, move inside the building toward a large, round chamber with a mirrored fire pit in its center and portraits of Luther Black on the walls. Shadowy figures move in this strange room and, as you approach, you realize they are Dark Hunters.

Dark Hunters will attack from the shadows.

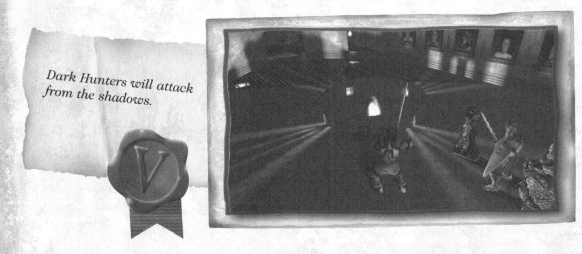

Dark Hunters

The Lasombra are a strange clan—they cast no reflection and it is whispered (though not in their presence) that they sold their souls to the devil and so gained this affliction. If they did sell their souls, they gained power indeed! Elder Lasombra can separate their very shadow from their flesh, creating spirit guardians called Dark Hunters. As spirits, these entities are vulnerable only to Aggravated and Elemental damage. Consequently, they are quite effective in their role as guards.

Fight your way through the room, making sure that you have destroyed all of the shadowy beasts. Search the alcoves on the walls and you'll find treasure—the Heart Shield and the Concoction!

Battling Dark Hunters

As spirits, Dark Hunters are very difficult to fight. Normal weapons will pass right through them. The best way to kill them is to use the discipline Feral Claws, which is possessed by both Wilhem and Erik. (It is possible that you have spent experience so that Christof has it, too.) Feral claws inflict tremendous Aggravated damage and can be used to send spirits back to the other side.

More Dark Hunters and ghouls guard the corridor outside the room. Some of the ghouls carry crossbows, and it is possible to get them to attack the Hunters—position yourself so that a Dark Hunter is between you and the ghouls. If the ghoul hits the Hunter and you have not yet attacked it, it will turn on the ghoul instead of you! Follow the corridor around to the stairs, then fight your way into the resting-place of Luther Black.

Luther rests on a cross of silver, looking up at a stained glass window showing Caine's expulsion from Eden. Unexpectedly, he does not want to fight you and begs you to kill him. He has been seeking the release of death for many years, but does not have the will to end his own life in sin. This is a difficult moral choice—you must decide if it is right for you to release Luther from his damnation. Should you deny his request, his anger gives him the impetus to do what he could not do alone: He opens the windows and sunlight floods the chamber! (It is quite possible that your coterie will not survive this, so perhaps it would be better to grant Luther's request.)

Accepting Luther's plea, shackle him, and then proceed up the stairs outside of his chamber. Here in the attic of the haven are two levers that will open the window to the direct light of the sun. You need to throw both levers at the same time to end Luther's tortured existence.

Cooperate to Solve

This is the first puzzle in which two characters must cooperate to succeed. Separate one member from the coterie (click on the green light next to their portrait) and move them next to one of the levers. Move the rest of the coterie close to the other lever. Use the separated character to throw the first lever, and then click or TAB over to the other characters to throw the second lever. (If you want to show off, use Celerity to move one character fast enough between the levers so that they can throw both within the time limit!)

The window opens and sunlight streams in, burning Luther to ash!

Quest Fulfilled: Kill Luther Black

Leave the haven, and turn back down the stairs. As you leave, Count Orsi and a group of Teutonic Knights will capture you—he has betrayed you!

Deutschordenskirche: Teutonic Knights Base

Enemies	Knights, Tremere, rats, spiders, hoppers
Boss	Dark Knight
Features	Some levers, lots of fighting
Treasure	Ainkurn Sword, Tremere amulet, lots of loot

Overview

The Deutschordenskirche is a vast fortress in the center of Vienna. From here the Teutonic Knights launch their crusade against the pagans and heretics of Eastern Europe and plan further conquests. Their base is a gothic fortress of dark stone with prison cells in the deep cellars, storerooms where they assemble resources for the war, and the famous chapel in the surface levels. Expect to fight every inch of the way in your escape from this bastion.

General Tactics

The Teutonic Knights can receive a great amount of punishment in their full plate armor. Indeed, their armor is so well made that it resists your feed attacks. They will attempt to overwhelm you with sheer numbers and crush your coterie's escape attempt. Luckily, four vampires are not helpless opponents. Aggravated damage will reduce the effectiveness of their armor, mental disciplines can shatter their resolve, and the sheer physical strength of Erik can break you out of dangerous situations.

Unbeknownst to the knights, the Tremere have been experimenting with enchantments on their armor. This keeps the knights alive for some moments after they should be dead—expect to face knights who can receive mortal wounds, even losing their heads, and still keep fighting you!

There is a great deal of loot in this level—probably more than you can carry out! The knights are preparing for war, so their storerooms are full of the resources they need. Feel free to take everything that you can. Not only do you profit, but you are striking a blow against an oppressive organization!

Some of the knights are on patrol, instead of guarding a specific location. Watch these knights so that you can fight them alone and cut them off from their comrades.

This level is a lot of fun—you get to use the full range of your vampiric powers against mortal enemies. Do not hesitate to demonstrate the powers of Caine to the fools who oppose you!

Navigating the Teutonic Knights Base

The fortress is a medieval castle—designed for easy defense. There are many switchback staircases and narrow corridors that will slow and confuse the enemy. It's also easy to get turned around in the gray stone chambers. It is best to move slowly through the level, taking note of any exits so that if you reach a dead-end, you can make your way back easily.

Teutonic Knights Base 4: The Dungeon

New Quest : Escape the Teutonic Knights Base

The coterie awakens in a dark cell in the depths of the fortress. Flickering torches light gray stone and the implements of torture fill many rooms. Orsi intends to starve you into submission, so it is time to organize a prison break. Serena will use her power to raise the dead and command a corpse to open the cell for you.

After the bars are open, kill the knights that rush to stop you. This level of the dungeon is made up of cellblocks overlooking a central pit (for the disposal of remains). Loot the cells opposite yours and proceed into the pit—another set of cells can be found here. As you move out of the cellblock, Serena mocks the knights who emerge to attack you.

Search the Prison Cells

The knights arrest and hurl their enemies into these cells to starve; but few of the knights care to search corpses for their possessions, so many items can be found abandoned there. Since the prisoners all died after the knights began their starvation policy, rats or poisonous spiders may also inhabit the cells.

Straight-ahead is a torture chamber. There's a battleaxe here that makes a fine weapon for Erik to wield. Follow the corridor to the left, fighting your way past the defenders until you enter another cellblock and a second torture room.

Stairs lead up from here, and the walls shift from gray to red stone as you come out on a platform overlooking the pit and cell where you were imprisoned. There are more cells here, monitored by more guardian knights. Force your way past them and find a round walkway that leads up through a portcullis into the storage rooms for the prison block. These rooms are now empty—the dead need no supplies. Beyond these rooms, stairs lead upward.

Teutonic Knights Base 3: Storage Facility

This level of the fortress is the main stockpile for the knights. Rooms full of crates and boxes hold the rations and other resources they need for their campaigns. Hidden here is the secret laboratory of the Tremere, separated from most of the knights who would mistrust the vampire sorcerers.

The stairs open into a wide hall. Straight-ahead is a storage room in which the knights will attempt to trap you, kill them to escape. Follow the ramp up, passing by an empty weapon rack (the knights here are alert to your presence and are fully armed), then enter the storage facility—four large rooms stacked high with crates.

Teutonic knights will attempt to ambush you here. Kill them all and search carefully for loot you can use. The exit is at the far side of the storeroom furthest from your entry point. Climb the stairs into yet another storeroom and emerge into a corridor that overlooks the beginning of the level. Slaughter the knights on duty here.

The corridor twists and turns before emerging onto a staircase. At the top is a Tremere warlock! Kill him and you'll see the coats-of-arms of both the knights and the warlocks—there is a conspiracy at work here. As you reach a locked portcullis, hoppers swarm out to attack you. Turning, you can see a Moorish arch that leads into a Tremere sanctum, lit by bale-fires and with stone trees growing from the walls.

Four more of the warlocks and their hopper servants attack you as you enter the room. Destroy them and enter the small antechamber. The gate swings shut behind you and you must fight a more powerful Tremere alone. He drops an Amulet when he dies; take it and the portcullis can be opened. (The Amulet has other secrets that will be revealed later.) Search the room and you'll find the precious Tome of Thaumaturgy: Lure of Flames. Beyond the portcullis, stairs lead up.

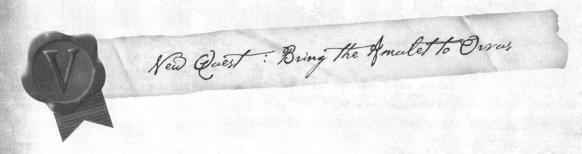

New Quest : Bring the Amulet to Orsus

Teutonic Knights Base 2: Heart of the Conspiracy

This is the lush headquarters of the knights and their Tremere allies. There is a deep blood-red carpet on the floor and murals cover the walls. Here the conspirators plan out their campaigns of conquest.

To your right, stairs lead into the main part of the level. Before you follow them, raid the storage rooms to the left and straight ahead. Both knights and the Tremere will oppose you, but there is much loot to be had. The four rooms each open from the main corridor, so take them one-by-one and dispose of your enemies in each.

When you return and climb the stairs, you are greeted by a beautiful mural and two hallways lined with statues of knights. Living knights also guard the hallways, which link again on the other side of the central chamber, so follow the one on the left. In the area behind the mural, you see a map of the city and the Tremere and Teutonic conspirators planning their campaign. Kill them and continue on, opposite the archway where you entered in a large chapel.

Upon entering, you are attacked by a group of knights—they are determined to keep you from this room.

Fight your way to the altar.

Kill them as you approach where the altar should be and you'll see a strange sword hanging from the wall. This is the Ainkurn Blade, a mighty artifact thought to have been lost in ages past. Seize it and prepare for a bloody vengeance on the knights!

Follow the long hall by the door to the Sword Chapel, then fight your way past the knights under the chandeliers to the exit.

Teutonic Knights Base 1: Deutschordenskirche

The ground level of the fortress has many spacious rooms with small chambers containing weapons and equipment to the sides. Part of it opens into a small courtyard under the night skies, and there is the famous Knight's Chapel where the Teutonic knights worship. Pillars and high ceilings rising above the brick walls characterize this area.

Climb upward, fighting your way through large, ornate rooms packed with knights. With the Ainkurn Sword in your hands they can do little to oppose you now. Continue to work your way upward until a door opens up into an outside courtyard. Stain the snow with the blood of the knights and go through the door into the final part of the building.

You pass through two armories with swords and pikes on weapon racks, and then enter the Church of the Knights. Instead of a priest, a Tremere is in the pulpit. Kill him and fight your way down the nave, battling the knights that emerge from the pews. Passing through a small vestry, you emerge into the main entranceway of the fortress.

A group of knights led by the Dark Knight makes a valiant attempt to stop you. A portcullis blocks the main doors of the fortress and no key is available.

Quest Fulfilled: Escape the Teutonic Knights Base

The main door opens onto the Inner Stradt. Go through the door to the east, then head into the Eastern Ring Strasse and take the Tremere Amulet to Orvus. He will be able to unlock its powers and gain you entrance to the Haus de Hexe.

Quest Fulfilled: Bring the Amulet to Orvus.
New Quest: Retrieve the Journal of Etrius

Return to your haven to save the game and spend experience, then make your way around to the Southern Ringstrasse. Pass through the double doors and go down the snow-covered path between high stone walls into the Haus de Hexe. With the Amulet in your possession, the way is clear and you can enter the Tremere stronghold.

Haus de Hexe

Enemies	Tremere, hoppers, gargoyles
Bosses	Virstania, Erik, Etrius
Features	Fireball traps, occult strangeness, the loss of Erik
Treasure	Tome of Ritual Thaumaturgy, strange blood, Berserker Fang, loot

Overview

The Haus de Hexe is a vast sandstone fortress devoted to blood magic—it is the heart of Clan Tremere and only the foolish or desperate would dare to attack it. Virtually all the walls are inscribed with occult symbols and the results of Tremere experimentation lie scattered everywhere.

General Tactics

The Tremere in the Haus are more dangerous than their fellow wizards in Prague. There is a greater percentage of older vampires here, so expect a tougher fight. The same basic principles apply—rush them so they cannot use their elemental powers, and destroy them when they run out of blood. Perhaps their most dangerous elemental power is Prison of Ice—this not only damages your characters, but also freezes them to the spot.

The Gargoyles are your most dangerous opponents here. They are the twisted products of Tremere alchemy and are deadly in battle. Made from tortured Cainite prisoners, these creatures embody all that is bestial about vampires. The only way to take out a gargoyle is to inflict tremendous damage on it as quickly as you can—just one of these beasts can easily slaughter your coterie.

Scattered throughout the chantry are enchanted statues that spew forth fire. Sometimes these can be avoided; other times you must rush past, hoping the flames miss you. Be especially careful if you are forced to retreat and forget that a firedog is there!

A mystical barrier seals Etrius' sanctum. To breach it, you will have to collect Arcanulum pieces from each of the levels and place them in the puzzle in the center of the main hall. Each piece is guarded at the end of the level. Luckily, a mystical gate will take you back to the hallway each time you claim a piece.

Because each level varies greatly in difficulty, you should probably clear the Library and Laboratory before you face the gargoyles. It would also be wise to return to your haven to save the game and spend experience before you enter the Lair.

Navigating the Haus de Hexe

The Library and the Laboratory are clearly laid out—central corridors and stairwells lead past a sequence of rooms. There are a few looping passages, but the way forward is always clear. The Gargoyle Lair is slightly different in that it is carved out of the stone of the hillside; many of the pathways switch back on themselves as they descend through rock. Whenever you enter a chamber, remember that the exit could be immediately behind you!

Stairs that lead up to Etrius' sanctum flank the main hallway of the Haus de Hexe—a mystical barrier seals this off. In the center of the floor is the Arcanulum Puzzle—pieces can found on each of the levels, which will unlock this and dissolve the mystical barrier. Across the chamber from the main entrance are three doors that lead to different areas of the chantry. Kill the three Tremere who guard the entrance and pick one of the doors.

Tremere Library

The Library is lit by a green light, demon faces leer at you from the walls, and the white stone is engraved with hermetic symbols. It is here that the Tremere conduct their ritual research, trying to define the powers of the blood and link them to hermetic theory. A single staircase connects all the studies and libraries within this level. Clear each room in turn as you progress downwards.

The first room to your left is a small study overlooking the stairwell; Tremere and hoppers come forth to attack you. Follow the staircase down to the first landing. Here three Tremere and their hoppers are working. Search the desks and corners of the shelves carefully as the Tremere have many scrolls, vials of blood, and valuable materials that they use in their research.

On the next landing is a small library with a conference room attached where the Tremere are holding a meeting to study a magical artifact. Slay them and seize the artifact—the Berserker Fang. The third landing opens up into a large supply room. Three Tremere are gathering supplies here and will stop work to attack you with their servants.

On the final landing is a large library with shelves reaching high up to the ceiling. More Tremere will gather to kill you and research your broken corpses.

Below this landing, the staircase ends in a small room with an inert magic circle and a treasure chest to one side.

To the right is a small reading room; kill the Tremere inside. The hallway splits around a stone pillar, leading into another library that contains an Arcanulum piece. Kill its guards and walk into the mystic portal behind it to return to the entranceway.

Tremere Laboratory

The Laboratory is lit by a pale blue light, which illuminates the dissections and the vivisection the Tremere are performing to perfect their knowledge of the body. Strange tortures and hideous alchemical experiments take place within these walls. The Tremere may seek knowledge, but they follow strange paths to do so.

The entrance to the Laboratory is lit by burning flames. To the right is a small reading room where the Tremere record the research. Introduce the Tremere here to a new experience. Stairs lead further into the area (these stairs have a firetrap on them, so it's easier to go back to the main entrance and take the left-hand path) and a raised walkway connects this room back to the entrance. The passage to the left leads downstairs into the Laboratory proper.

A corpse is crucified here and the Tremere are studying its internal organs. Fight the Tremere and search for any blood they may have taken from their victim.

The crucifixion room

Stairs lead down past a fireball trap; run past it carefully, then head into another chamber. This one has a pit in the center of the floor where body parts and blood are collected. Kill the warlocks and proceed up the small staircase (the longer staircase leads back up to the reading room).

In the next room, an alchemical alembic is lit by bale-fire as the Tremere attempt to purify and modify Cainite blood. Kill the alchemists and search the alembic carefully. You will find much potent blood, including a sample of Giant's Blood. Save this precious vitae for when you desperately need it.

Both exits from this alchemical laboratory lead to the same room; however, the staircase on the left is free of traps and leads to another research room. Kill the Tremere and search for useful scrolls, then choose either of the two exits. The staircase that is slightly lower leads into a room where Tremere necromancers are experimenting with reanimating dead tissue. Here the warlocks have been studying the Tome of Thaumaturgy Rituals. Reclaim this treasure, then head back to the research room and take the other staircase.

In this last laboratory, the wall is taken up entirely by a hanging frame on which prisoners are vivisected and studied. Samples of blood can be found here, including Fae and Antediluvian vitae, which are used by the Tremere for comparative experiments. Follow the exit around and into a long corridor.

This leads into the room holding the Arcanulum piece. The piece is on a raised dais flanked by statues of gargoyles; the mystic portal is behind it. Fight your way up to it and leave the cursed laboratories behind.

Take Precautions

Before attempting the Gargoyle Lair, it would be wise to return to your haven and save the game, as well as spend experience. You can also visit the shops of Vienna to equip your coterie and purchase new equipment.

Gargoyle Lair

The Gargoyle Lair has been carved out of the side of the hill the Haus is built into. Here Virstania, Mistress of Gargoyles, trains her charges and seeks to understand their potent blood potential. In the gargoyle nests, you can find the remains of their victims, treasure carelessly cast aside, and the potent blood that the Tremere use to continue refining their servants.

The opening of the Lair is carved from white stone like the rest of the Haus, with red bale-fire casting an eerie glow over the walls. Three Tremere occupy a small storeroom to the left and the corridor soon opens up to a canyon under the snowy skies. Here, a lone Tremere will try to block your progress. Follow the tunnel in the canyon wall deep into the rock. As the passage climbs, a single gargoyle stands ready to eat any intruders. Follow the small tunnel that slopes sharply up to the right and you'll find some forgotten treasures.

Follow the main tunnel into a gargoyle nest where three gargoyles and their warlock master will attack you. In their feeding pens you can find the remains of unlucky prisoners as well as some treasure and blood.

The exit from this nest is next to the tunnel you came in along. Follow it down, fighting the gargoyles at the bottom, and then enter another nest with two more gargoyles and Tremere. This nest contains Werewolf vitae, a potent brew that the Tremere have been using to increase the power of the gargoyles. Once again, the exit is adjacent to the entry and the tunnel continues to plunge into the earth.

Fight two more gargoyles and you'll emerge into a large room where Virstania and her favorite gargoyle defend the Arcanulum piece. Kill them both and pass through the portal into the entrances of the Haus.

When you place this final piece into the Arcanulum puzzle, Etrius' mystical barrier will dissolve and you can enter his sanctum.

Etrius' Sanctum

Etrius' sanctum is above the main entrance of the Haus. A vast domed chamber with the night skies visible above, here the master of the Haus performs his rituals and researches the strange events, which plague both the clan and its founder. Etrius is often a troubled man, lamenting the loss of magic and the damnation of the vampiric condition. He finds little comfort in the bleak night sky.

His journal rests on a small book-lined niche just inside the entrance to his sanctum. Taking the journal alerts Etrius who teleports in to confront you. He uses his powerful magic to complete Erik's transformation into a gargoyle, finally forcing you to fight your friend.

Erik the Gargoyle

Type	Transformed Ancient Gangrel
Description	As the warlock's magic warps Erik's blood, he transforms into a powerful gargoyle. His red hair and beard become a leonine mane while his powerful body twists into a monstrous form and wings sprout from his shoulder blades.
Health	200
Soak	0/0/0
Damage	100 A
Powers	None
Weaknesses	The creature that once was Erik is in a bestial rage. It will not use disciplines against you.
Tactics	Erik the Gargoyle is in a bestial frenzy and you have no choice except to destroy him. He will concentrate his attacks on whomever hurts him the most, so use this to your advantage—make sure the first member of your coterie to attack him is the best armored and, therefore, able to stand toe-to-toe with Erik. The gargoyle will concentrate his attacks on that one person, leaving the others free to act.

67

Etrius transforms Erik into a Gargoyle.

Once you have defeated Erik, Etrius will attempt to kill you himself. Tiring of the fight, he gives you the information you need and escapes.

Etrius of the Council of Seven

Type	Insanely Powerful Vampire Sorcerer
Description	Nothing prepared Etrius for eternity, and weariness shows in every line of his immortal face and body. He wears plain robes, preferring that his power show through without the need for ostentatious dress. His eyes reveal all one needs to know of damnation.
Health	200
Soak	30/30/30 +30 Soak vs. Fire, Electricity, and Cold
Damage	85 A
Powers	Etrius possesses all the powers of the lesser Tremere, but with centuries of experience, first as a mortal mage and now as the undead. His ability to manipulate the elements and the minds of his foes is unsurpassed (Feed 3, Blood Healing 3, Theft of Vitae 3, and Call Lightning 3).
Weaknesses	Etrius does not have time to deal with the intrusion. When the coterie's resistance proves stronger than expected, he will depart.
Tactics	Once Etrius starts spell casting, you have little chance. The best way to defeat him is to keep him constantly off-guard with melee attacks.

Theorizing the Storyline

How did Christof defeat Etrius, the Tremere Methuselah? The simple answer is because Etrius does not have the power to spare to destroy the coterie. He has many concerns and crushing upstarts is not high on the list. Your resistance proved that it would be costly for him to destroy you, so he chooses to send you on your way. A second theory would be that Tremere is not away from the Chantry, but rather fighting the other being which haunts Clan Tremere. If this is the case, then Etrius is needed urgently and literally has neither the time nor the power to fight you.

You will find the remains of Erik's equipment off to one side of the room. Leave sadly, and make your way back to Orvus of the Order of Hermes. He congratulates you and casts an enchantment on you that will help protect you in combat!

Quest Fulfilled: Retrieve the Journal of Etrius
New Quest : Return to Prague

Return to the desecrated church where you have made your haven. The gate is now open and you can return to Prague through it.

Quest Fulfilled: Return to Prague

Prague: Devil's Night

Your coterie arrives in Prague outside of the East Gate. In the distance you can hear shouts and screams. Enter town and you'll realize that something has gone horribly wrong—fires are burning everywhere and fallen masonry and makeshift barricades block many of the streets.

New Quest : Visit Ecaterina

Enter the University and Ecaterina will explain that the conflict between the clans and between mortal and immortal has erupted into full-scale war while you have been gone. You must defy her wishes, and instead follow Anezka into the heart of the battle at Vysehrad Castle. Go into your haven and save the game to prepare for this great battle.

Quest Fulfilled: Visit Ecaterina
New Quest : Infiltrate Vysehrad Castle

Fires and tumbled stone block all the paths in Prague, except for the one that leads to the Vysehrad Acropolis. The gate is behind the Convent. Take it and follow the mountain path up to the crumbling castle, past the hoard of peasants and townsfolk who seek to tear down their vampiric overlords.

Vysehrad Castle

Enemies	Revenants, rats, wolves, szlachta, war ghouls, lesser Vozhd, Tzimisce
Boss	Vozhd
Features	The defilement of Anezka, a meeting with the Voivode, Tome of Hands of Destruction
Loot	None that matters

Overview

Vysehrad Castle has dominated the skyline of Prague since time immemorial, but now… no longer. The acropolis of the Tzimisce Voivode Vukodlak is in shambles. The peasants have stormed the castle and all is in ruins. The once mighty fortress is now crumbling and aflame. You will have to force your way past the debris and destruction to find the deep cellars and catacombs where evil sleeps.

General Tactics

The enemies of this level are broken and in disarray. This gives your coterie the advantage. Many of their finest warriors have already been slain, so you face their rag-tag last stand. Do not underestimate the power of the Tzimisce, however—these twisted vampires warp weapons out of their own flesh and can command the souls of beasts and men alike.

In any battle, take out the Tzimisce first—one of their most common attacks is to drive their enemies into a frenzy and let the Beast do their killing for them. Should one of your coterie fall into a frenzy, move the other characters away from them so you are not in the path of their rage.

With the power your coterie possesses and the equipment you have won for yourselves along the way, you should have little trouble clearing out this castle. The only true challenge is the lesser Vozhd that waits in the lower levels.

Little treasure that is worth collecting remains in the castle. The most important things to find are the Discipline Tome and the various council proclamations that explain how Vukodlak came to his present, fallen state.

The Tzimisce are proud of the wolves they breed as guards and pets. If any of your characters has developed the Animalism discipline, you can turn these servants against their masters.

Navigating the Acropolis

The castle, which would once have presented a maze of rooms, is now falling about you. Many pathways are blocked off and your coterie must work their way around the destruction to find the paths leading downward.

Vysehrad Castle 1: Castle in Flames

The higher levels of the castle are on fire, so it pays to hurry through them to avoid being caught in the conflagration. Beneath the wreckage you can see what a magnificent fortress Vysehrad Castle once was.

In the grand hallway of the castle, burning beams crash to the floor. Three Tzimisce attack you in frenzy, but you should be able to dispatch them with ease. A grand staircase sweeps above the main floor; should you claim it, you can find some rats and a little treasure. A side room to the left contains more rats and other treasures left in the panic.

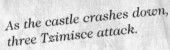

As the castle crashes down, three Tzimisce attack.

To the right, revenants and Tzimisce are preparing to make a last stand in a storeroom. Kill them and carefully descend the broken staircase. The storerooms on this level are in disarray—beams have fallen from the ceiling and fire threatens to break out everywhere. Work your way through the wreckage, fighting off war ghouls, szlachta, and rats, then find the stairs.

Continue down the stairs and into a corridor guarded by wolves, then fight the Tzimisce lurking in another ruined room. The corridor winds its way around past a group of revenants herding a war ghoul to the castle's defense. Past these defenders, frantic rats and doomed szlachta hide in a storeroom. The stairs lead down to the next level.

Vysehrad Castle 2: Tzimisce Lair

This part of the castle was the lair of the Tzimisce servants of the Voivode. It was here that they practiced their dark rituals and studied the ancient works of koldunic sorcery. Although not as badly damaged as the upper level, this part of the castle shows signs of collapse, forcing the coterie to fight through many rooms.

The main balcony and stairs on this level have been shattered by falling debris. Follow the open path along the balcony, fighting off the war ghoul and szlachta. Szlachta and their larger cousin hold another supply room; kill them then follow the stairs down.

At the bottom of the stairs to your left is a koldunic shrine where the Tzimisce call on dark spirits. Kill the fiends within and lay claim to the Tome of Thaumaturgy Hands of Destruction, then kill the wolves guarding the antechamber, checking it for any treasure.

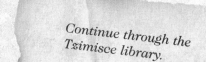

Hands of Destruction

The discipline Hands of Destruction can be used only by vampires with a low humanity score. If you have been a hero during your quests, its powers will be unavailable to you. However, if you have followed a more selfish path, you can make good use of its secrets.

Continuing down, you enter the castle library. The Tzimisce have nailed one of the townsfolk to the wall to aid their concentration.

Continue through the Tzimisce library.

Kill them and their revenant slaves, then continue to fight your way down the corridor, checking the rooms to the side for enemies and treasure. A war ghoul blocks your progress down the corridor and a passage leads downward to the prison cells. Climb the stairs up to the main balcony and follow the shattered stairs down to the main floor. Kill the rat swarm there and go through the doors.

Vysehrad Castle 3

Deep underground, this level still shakes from the destruction wrought above. Although the core foundations remain, solid stonework—including a massive pillar—have fallen. Some Tzimisce carvings remain visible in the stone floors and walls as you near your destination.

On a balcony overlooking a large hall, go to your right and deal with the Tzimisce who has been gathering his treasures. Loot them and then go to the left along the balcony, fighting off the wolves, then climb down the broken stone pillar to the floor.

Four Tzimisce have rallied to their castle's defense, so expect a hard fight as they attack whoever comes down the pillar first. After dispatching them, take the stairs down to a small antechamber. Kill the wolves guarding a pitiful pile of treasure, then push open the large double doors.

In this vast chamber with its elaborately patterned floor and burning fires, a Vozhd defends the crypt of its master. This massive creature can consume a vampire whole and presents a tough battle.

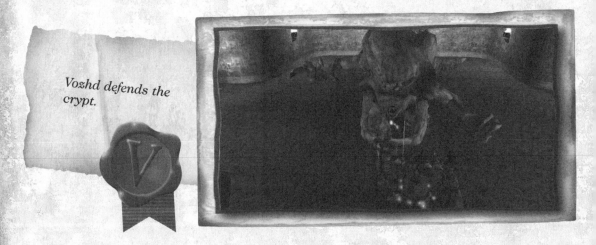

Vozhd defends the crypt.

Once it's dead, the doors can be opened and you can enter the crypt of the Voivode.

Vysehrad Castle 4: The Crypt of the Voivode

This vast underground chamber is the scene of your confrontation with Anezka, Libussa, and the sleeping Vukodlak. As you walk into the crypt, a cutscene will begin and the castle will collapse about you.

London

Before beginning the detailed strategy of the London segment of your adventure, let's briefly discuss each area you'll encounter.

Starting Out

Christof starts in the basement of the Society Level 3 and works his way up to Level 1 where he will met Father Leo of the Society of Leopold. You will have a choice to either kill him or break his vats of blood. Once this is completed you can exit the Society and enter the London Hub.

London Hub

The next scene begins with Christof still in dark ages clothing, standing outside of the Society of Leopold. Proceed down the street directly in front of Christof, making a left at the "T" intersection. Christof will be accosted by a mugger at this point, and should end up in his modern day outfit after the conversation. You may freely visit the rest of the hub, but most links at this point will be closed. Find Club Tenebrae and enter it. Inside you will find Pink. Talk to him and, after the conversation, he will have joined your party.

Pink Tour

Now that you have Pink in your party, a few more links will have opened up throughout the hub. You may visit Sumner in the Curio Shop in West London now. Pink will update you on the modern world at various points during your travels. In East London, if you head down to Otto, beneath the bridge, a few enlightening scenes will occur between Chris and Pink. At some point, you'll need to visit the Setite Brothel. The entrance is located in an alley next to the abandoned looking theatre directly in front of the Underground entrance.

Brothel

Just inside the entrance to the Brothel, you'll find Lily. Click on her and after a brief conversation, she will join your party and give you a clue about where you need to go next. Proceed to the back of the Brothel, and there you will find the entrance to the Setite Temple below. (Throw the lever to open the door.)

Setite Temple

Your party enters the secret entrance from the Brothel, which takes them to an underground Egyptian lair controlled by the Setites. The players make their way down four levels to meet Lucretia. Exit this level and head to the Tower of London next.

Tower of London

Head over to the Tower of London and proceed throughout the levels. At the top of the tower you will find Lucretia's Heart. After retrieving it, you will need to return to lower level of the Setite Temple. A conversation with the guard just outside of the Temple's entrance will jump you straight down to the lower level.

The Bartering

Now that you have Lucretia's Heart, you have some bargaining power. Walk through the level until you see Lucretia, and walk up the stairs to stand in front of her. A conversation will start, after which you will need to kill her. During the course of the conversation the party learns of a ship leaving for New York called the St. Magdalena. When Lucretia is badly wounded, her servant will drop the heart (which has been handed to him by Pink). Pick the heart up and kill Lucretia, then head back to the London Hub. When you get there, head down to the docks and enter the ship via the ramp leading up to it.

Cargo Ship

Head down to the docks area and board the St. Magdalena. Once aboard, walk between the stacks of crates and you'll find the murdered Interpol agents. Kill the Sabbat vampires and you'll be transported to the New York Hub.

The Awakening

Eight centuries have passed since the fall of Vysehrad Castle and Christof has slumbered through them all. Awakened from torpor by a mysterious voice, he finds himself alone in the modern age—unarmed, friendless, and in the heart of an enemy's stronghold. Good luck, crusader!

Welcome to London

The sun has truly set on the heart of the Empire; London is a city of ancient buildings and modern corruption. A steady supply of drugs and armaments moved through the city by the Setites, and Giovanni has corrupted the once great metropolis. Still there is light in the endless night. You will find new allies for your journey and perhaps seek redemption in the New World.

Society of Leopold

Enemies	Soldiers, lab workers
Boss	Father Leo
Features	A test of might between an elder vampire and modern firepower
Treasure	Modern weapons, loot

Overview

The Society of Leopold is the direct descendent of the Inquisition, acting with only partial sanction from the church, they continue their centuries' old crusade against the creatures of the night. The lower levels of their base contain weapons storage and training facilities, as well as the scientific resources they use to analyze captured Cainites. These levels are spartan and functional with a uniform, institutional bleakness. The upper level is disguised behind a Georgian Townhouse on a quiet London terrace, and is lushly furnished with the trophies of many successful expeditions.

General Tactics

While vampires are fairly resistant to damage, the Society of Leopold are well trained in their mission. In addition to guns and whatever weapons the workers can find at hand, their soldiers carry stakes and use flame-throwers regularly. Such weapons directly impact vampiric vulnerabilities and can be deadly to you. Make sure you can disable or destroy the wielders of such weapons immediately.

Mortal training has its limits and you should use your powers to their fullest extent on this level— the members of the Society are only mortal after all and you should remind them of this fact. Also, you can burn blood freely as each enemy on this level is the source of more vitae for you!

It is possible to fight each soldier individually and simply destroy them, but it's more fun to use a range of powers, feeding between each bout of combat. Mental control disciplines will scatter groups of foes, Obfuscate will hide you from their sight, and Fortitude will render you immune to their attacks. The possibilities are endless—use them!

The most dangerous thing about fighting these fanatics is the power of True Faith. Once this power has been activated, any 'unholy' creature that comes close to the fanatic is damaged by the power of faith itself. You can tell if a Society of Leopold member has activated this power by the faint glow that surrounds him. The damage that the aura of Faith does to you makes it impossible to feed upon them and dangerous to use disciplines such as Mesmerize, which would draw them close. Instead, destroy the Society workers and soldiers at range using other disciplines or modern firearms so that you always remain at a safe distance.

Rather than the chests and coffins you looted in previous locations, treasure is now kept in footlockers, crates, suitcases, and other modern paraphernalia. Don't overlook any of these sources of equipment, because you start the modern day unarmed and nearly naked.

At various points in the level you can find journal entries, computer e-mail messages, and other information that fill in the last eight centuries. Make sure that you read these documents so that you can understand what has happened since Devil's Night in Prague.

Navigating the Society of Leopold

The underground bunker of the Society is an exercise in efficiency. A central corridor connects all the rooms on each level. Simply follow the corridor to its end and you'll find the exit to each level, which is conveniently marked with a neon sign! You should, however, investigate each side-room to make sure that you have destroyed all the vampire hunters and properly equipped yourself for the Modern Nights.

Society of Leopold 3

You awaken in the lower levels of the Society's London headquarters. Here, deep underground, they work to catalogue the finds from Eastern Europe. Dour gray corridors connect laboratories and store rooms.

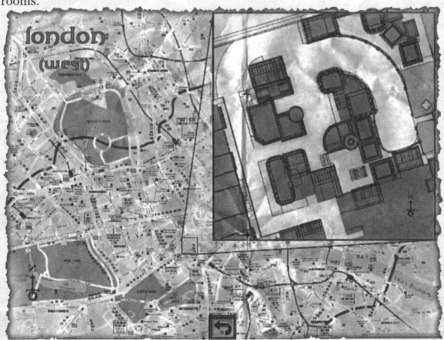

Battling Summoned Creatures

Many vampires can summon other creatures to fight with them—ranging from the mundane, such as rats, up to wraiths and elementals. In general, it is best to ignore the summoned creature as it has only a temporary existence. Instead, concentrate on the vampiric master who can, in any case, summon more creatures. Later in the game you will be able to summon your own allies.

You begin in a loading bay where you quickly overwhelm the lone worker. Search the room to find a pistol and blood. When you're ready, open the door and proceed up the stairs. Three more workers will attempt to sound the alarm; silence them and search the second storeroom for more weapons. A door opens into a long hallway.

Modern Weapons and Vampires

For all a vampire's resistance to damage, modern weapons can be surprisingly dangerous. Firearms allow a foe to attack you at long distances, and weapons that use fire or explosions can easily put you into torpor. To avoid such trauma, always be aware of which weapons your foes are carrying and destroy those most dangerous to you first.

This central hall is patrolled by soldiers; rush up to them or use your mental disciplines to call them to you. Before you proceed down the hallway, go through the door opposite the storeroom exit and enter a computer room connected to a biology laboratory. Defeating the workers, you can find blood amongst the medical tools.

Defeat the workers in the laboratory.

Go back into the hallway and, at the first branch, kill the soldiers and loot both of the locker rooms that can be found here. Both of these rooms are guarded, but you can find treasure (including a modern flashlight) if you search the metal racks.

Go to the end of the hallway where a sealed blast door blocks your way. Kill the soldiers guarding the side corridor and go through the door. Here in a second loading bay you can find a switch that will open the blast doors, allowing you to progress further. The workers and soldiers in this loading bay have not heard the noise outside so you can surprise them and search the room for useful equipment. One of the things you find is a satchel charge.

Using Explosives

Explosives are a deadly product of modern warfare and come in many forms—from demolition charges to various grenades. All of these weapons are thrown and can either be equipped in the character's weapon hand or placed in Quick Item slots. When such a thrown weapon is activated, a targeting cursor will appear on-screen, allowing you to chose where you want to throw the device. Be careful, most explosives do damage in a radius and you or your allies may be caught in the blast!

Leave the loading bay and go through the blast doors—the corridor bears right. Enter the first door you find and kill the soldiers and worker cataloguing the Society's finds. Go back into the corridor and past an alcove with a computer workstation and giant sample freezers. The next door off of the hall leads into a cellblock—kill the soldiers guarding it and use the levers on the wall to open and search the cells. These cells have held Kindred prisoners and you may find something of use.

Go back into the hall and fight your way past the soldiers that guard it. A door leads into a hazardous material store. Past it are the stairs leading up, guarded by a single worker.

Society of Leopold 2: Center of Operations

This level is as functional as the last, but more densely populated. Here you will find the various research labs of the Society, as well as their library and a shooting range. Explore these areas carefully—there is much that may be of use in your quest.

Leaving the small locker room where you started, exit into a large corridor. Avoid and kill the guards, then head straight ahead into a storeroom guarded by workers and soldiers. Kill them and then take the left branch of the corridor. The corridor leads to an intersection guarded by soldiers.

If you turn left at the intersection, you'll find three doors. The first leads into a shooting gallery where you can find a new weapon and more ammunition. The second is sub-generator for the complex; unfortunately, you have neither the knowledge nor the ability to disable the building's power. The third room leads into a medical bay where injured Society members' wounds are treated; you can replenish your blood supply here. All of these rooms are guarded, but you can easily overwhelm the occupants with surprise and a demonstration of vampire power.

Turn right at the intersection and you'll come to a door. The corridor then presents a dead-end with a second door. Through the first door is an emptied armory where a single worker is taking stock. The second door leads into a medical containment facility (a hot zone). A small, clean room leads into the larger containment facility. Several workers are attempting to analyze the infectious properties of Kindred blood here and you can find supplies.

Follow the corridor straight and it soon turns. You'll reach a door to the left that's guarded by two soldiers. This leads into the Operations Center where three soldiers are making plans. Kill them and continue onward. The next doors along the wall lead into the Society's extensive library of occult materials. Three workers and two soldiers are studying the dusty grimoires. Kill them and find a prize—the Tome of Thaumaturgy Lure of Flames! (If you have already learned this discipline, save the Tome for a coterie member who does not have this power!)

The Society's library

The corridor continues past a guard to a T-junction. To the left are two doors that lead into bunkrooms where workers can sleep. Further down, the corridor widens and is used as a storage space for large crates and supplies—several soldiers and workers have set an ambush for you here.

Battle Tactics

Since you are directly outnumbered in this area with little opportunity to pick off lone humans, use a display of your vampire powers to break up the ambush. Either attack them individually while protected by Obfuscate or use mental commands to turn them against each other. You can even activate Fortitude or Blood Stamina and rely on your vampire resistance to save you in a direct fight.

Opposite this ambush site, two doors lead into a science laboratory and a storeroom. Kill the workers within and then go up the stairs to the ground floor of the complex.

Society of Leopold 1: London Townhouse

This lushly appointed Georgian townhouse is the pride of the Society of Leopold. Here members can discus past conquests while relaxing in elegant surroundings, including cabinets full of prized trophies and treasures of British art. The calm of this setting has been shattered by your arrival and armed soldiers stand ready to repel your escape attempt.

Hit the switch on the wall of the small wooden room where you start—this will open the door into the morning room of the mansion's ground floor. Four soldiers will attempt to gun you down and the doors to the outside world are securely locked. Follow the staircase that leads up to the second floor.

A soldier guards the double doors at the top of the stairs; kill him and open them. Walk down the carpeted hallway, taking in the art treasures and killing the soldiers. Double doors lead off the corridor into a trophy room and its adjoining study. Several soldiers guard these treasures.

Continue down the hallway as it turns, then kill the guards and enter a second trophy room; in one of the cases is the mystical artifact—the Argent Baton!

Dispatch all the soldiers and search for anything that may be use in the opened cabinet. Down the hall, soldiers and workers hide behind more glass-fronted cabinets and will try to ambush you. Opposite them is a wide open space—Father Leo Allatius' study. Sneak past the study to the double doors at the end of the hall. Kill the soldiers who are readying their weapons in here and return to the study.

Here you confront Father Leo Allatius, a centuries old ghoul, who has been using the Society's vampire hunts to supply him with vitae. You can either fight him directly or shatter his precious blood vats, plunging the old man into despair.

Father Leo Allatius

Type	Ghoul Fanatic
Description	Father Leo appears as a man in his late middle age. However, he is actually over two centuries old, having sustained himself on the blood of slain vampires. He is fanatically devoted to the Society and fails to see the redemptive chance in Christof.
Health	100
Soak	0/0/0
Damage	55 B
Powers	Father Leo is far stronger than any normal human and greatly skilled with his staff/walking cane.
Weaknesses	Leo is addicted to kindred blood that he keeps stored in vast vats in his study. If you destroy the vats, he will collapse helplessly.
Tactics	When it comes down to it, Father Leo is merely mortal. Christof is an elder vampire at this point, so use your powers or your physical prowess to overwhelm him.

Once you have dealt with Allatius, go back downstairs. A door from the morning room is now open. Fight your way past the soldiers and leave the vampire hunters behind you.

The streets of London are dark and rainy with a few brave pedestrians facing the storm. Proceed down the hill along the terraced street. You will encounter a mugger and have the opportunity to dress in the modern style. After you have seen this villain off, continue to follow the road down the hill. You pass by a shop, Magpie Curios, which you can return to later.

Follow the buildings at the bottom of the hill until you see a neon sign: Club Tenebrae. Enter the club and go to the bar where you meet Pink, a fellow Brujah.

New Quest : Infiltrate Setite Lair

Exit the Club with Pink and listen to his view of modern life. Go up the narrow alley beside the club to the street at the top of the hill. With Pink alongside you, you can now enter Magpie Curios and sell any loot you have from the Society. Sumner Monatague is a strange fellow who recognizes you for what you are, but still does business with you. Perhaps the sign of his shop will give you clue as to what he really is…

Turn left as you leave the shop and follow the street through the concrete posts. These stairs lead down to a London Underground station.

Mind the Gap

The London Underground is the transportation system that links the metropolis. You can use it to travel between West London and the East End docks. With Pink at your side, you will not be bothered on your journey.

You emerge from the underground station on the other side of the city. Almost straight ahead of you stone steps lead down to the docks and London Bridge. Take these steps (on the first platform turn right to go directly to the docks) all the way down to the river embankment. Out of a seemingly abandoned van, Pink's friend Otto runs an illegal gun shop—buy what modern weaponry you can afford. Close to Otto's van, in the base of London Bridge, is an access door that leads into your haven. Go through the door and save the game. Follow the embankment around the base of the bridge and you'll reach the entrance to the Tower of London—you will return here later.

The entrance to your haven is close to Otto's van.

Leave your haven, climb back up the stairs, and follow the street around the corner. A large theatre stands in fading glory, seemingly boarded up and abandoned. Walk to the side of the theatre where you can climb the stairs and enter through the stage door into the Setite Brothel!

Lily joins the coterie.

The insides of the old theatre have been renovated and devoted to pleasure—Art Deco lamps light the way and the floors are heavily carpeted. Just inside is a prostitute who will make pink an offer he can't refuse. You soon meet Lily, a Toreador singer, who is trapped in the brothel. Lily joins your coterie and gives you a clue as to the location of the Setite Temple.

Follow the corridor around the corner, past another prostitute and her john, then go into a crowded junk room. Egyptian styled paraphernalia surrounds you, but you must search for a lever against the side wall. Throw the lever and one painting slides up, revealing the entrance to the Temple!

Quest Fulfilled: Infiltrate Setite Lair

Temple of Set

Enemies	Setites, snakes
Boss	Lucretia
Features	Several traps, lots of levers, lobster pot rooms
Treasure	Black gloves, chainsaw, modern weapons

Description

Tunneling deep beneath the Theatre façade, the Setites have built a vast Egyptian temple in honor of their dark god, Set, under the center of London. Frescoes and statues celebrate the life of the dark one and the entire perfect replicas of Egyptian locations make it seem as if the coterie has stepped back five millennia.

General Tactics

The Setites are vicious foes. With a combination of modern military weapons and ancient arts, they will pound your coterie mercilessly. The most deadly carry rocket launchers, but almost all of them are armed to one degree or another. The most dangerous feature in fighting the Setites is their use of mental disciplines to disable opponents. Expect to find coterie members standing helplessly enthralled as your enemies close in.

The best method to fight back against these monsters is to hit them harder than they hit you—a group of them can easily overwhelm you, so use your disciplines to disable them before they can surround you. You will often be able to attack one of your foes before they see you and raise the alarm, so use that opportunity to take them out. Be swift and brutal in your attacks if you hope to survive!

Make sure that all members of your coterie are supplied with blood and ammunition for their weapons. Following the principle that the best defense is a strong offense, use all means at your disposal to overwhelm the serpents.

Navigating the Temple

The Temple is an exceedingly complicated level; opening most doors requires you to find the corresponding lever or switch, and then set out across the temple, fighting its guardians as you try to open doors. This involves a lot of doubling back, so it's important for you to kill every enemy in any location before proceeding onward. There are also several hidden rooms and many secrets to be discovered!

Setite Temple 1: Temple of Smoke

Like the rest of the Temple, this level has been constructed to match the wonders of ancient Egypt. Flickering fires light the murals of ancient times and statues and elaborately decorated columns are everywhere. The Setites keep the Temple feverishly hot to keep their reptilian friends happy; the air is full of smoke and incense.

Walk down the narrow steps beneath high flanking stone buttresses and throw open the doors. A large room with a statue of Set killing Osiris confronts you and the large door straight ahead is locked. Go to your left and follow the corridor into a small chamber dominated by a mural of Set. Kill the Setites and search for loot, then return to the large room and take the exit to the left.

This mural of Set dominates the small chamber.

In another chamber there are several Setite warriors and a lever that will open the great door. Go back and through the newly opened door, then head down the stairs and fight the two Setites who emerge into another corridor. To the right is another secured door, so go left down the corridor.

Fight your way down the corridor, past Setites guarding strange snake-shaped cauldrons (check behind them for loot). Climb the steps into a room where you will find another lever and more serpents.

Battling Groups of Enemies

In the midst of battle, especially with modern weapons, a lot of things can go wrong. Always make sure that you have enemies between you and any foe using heavy weapons—there's a good chance that your foes' attacks will harm each other! In battle, always be aware of the position of your coterie and all your enemies. This will give you a great tactical advantage.

Pull the lever to open the locked door, then return the way you came. Beyond the locked door is a large chamber, its sides lined with alcoves. A group of six Setites will emerge from the alcoves to attack you here, so hit them hard. Stairs continue down to the right, but there is a secret to be discovered first!

Look into the last alcove on the left. Near the floor is a hidden switch. Throw it and a wall panel will slide up. Climb the newly revealed staircase into a secret chamber. Two vipers guard many treasures, including the Black Gloves!

Go back down the stairs and continue downward until you reach a large room full of square, Egyptian styled pillars. Eight Setites will attack you using assault rifles and stake guns.

Using Your Environment

This can be a difficult fight, so use the pillars to your advantage, ducking for cover and engaging the Setites individually. Firearms only work if they have a clear line-of-sight, so prevent the Setites from getting a clear bead on you by moving around the pillars and blocking their shots. As any Setites armed with melee weapons close in on you, they may well be hit by their comrades.

After you've beaten the guards, go through the engraved doors to the next level.

Setite Temple 2: Temple of Fire

This section of the Temple seems devoted to fire—there are several traps set to burn your coterie and the section is lit by many burning braziers and wall sconces. The Egyptian theme continues to be dominated with the white-washed walls decorated by murals and Setite symbols.

At the start of this level you face a wooden bridge over a pit of fire. Sprint across the bridge, avoiding the fireballs that launch from the fires below and traps in the walls.

Avoid the fire as you cross the bridge.

Go either left or right (the paths reconnect in the next room), and then throw the lever in the small antechamber after overcoming the guard. Each lever opens the door in the opposite room, so run back over the bridge into the second antechamber. Throw the other lever to keep your options open, then go down the ornate staircase into a large room that contains a minor shrine to Set.

Setites and vipers attempt to stop your defilement of this holy place. To the right there is a sealed door, so climb the steps to the left and kill the Setites in the corridor. Follow this around until you come upon another fire pit—this one is blocked by a heavy portcullis. Kill the Setites and the snakes basking in the heat of the flames, then walk around the edge of the fire pit to the left and into a lavishly decorated room where six Setites will try to destroy you.

Splash Damage

These Setites are heavily armed, including the first foe you face with a grenade launcher. Grenades, and later rockets, do a tremendous amount of damage to their target, as well as to all those who surround it. The only way to avoid this damage is to avoid getting hit, so either move very quickly to avoid the shots, or destroy the weapon's user.

After the fight, loot the shrine and throw the lever here that will open the portcullis over the fire pit. Return to the fire pit and sprint across it to trigger the floor plate at its end. A section of the wall opposite you will slide up, revealing another shrine guarded by two Setites and their snakes. In the shrine is the Tome of Obfuscate and a lever that will open the sealed door in the main chamber.

Go back there and proceed through the newly unlocked door. Two Setites with grenade launchers will try to stop you. Further down the corridor, at a junction, two more Setites will ambush you. Kill them and open the engraved door, which slides up into the ceiling to reveal a pillared chamber beyond.

As soon as you enter this room the door slides shut behind you, quite possibly trapping the rest of your coterie outside. Four Setites will try to kill you in here, and you must defeat them to open the doors. After you have won, open the second door out of the room and fight your way through another identical room, this one with six heavily armed Setite warriors!

Wait for two more Setites in the small antechamber, then kill them and descend the stairs.

Setite Temple 3: Serpentine Shrine

This level of the shrine is devoted to the Setites' serpent friends. A large chamber at the center of the level is a breeding pit for the vipers where they can bask and hatch their eggs in warmth and safety. There are many heavily armed Setite warriors, as well as their vipers, across this level.

Warriors ambush you as soon as you enter the first great chamber of this level. They are using grenades and are dedicated to defending their hatchery from you.

Warrior Ambush!

The best way to avoid an ambush is to come through from the previous level with defensive disciplines activated. Celerity can enable you to move before the Setites fire, and Fortitude will help you resist the damage. If you have access to Obfuscate, coming into the level invisible will prevent the Setites from attacking you.

After the smoke from the battle clears, you can see that there are two doors leaving this chamber and stairs leading up. Climb the stairs as the doors are barred, and follow the narrow platform around to a balcony overlooking the snake hatchery. Kill the guards on the balcony and throw the switches in the wall, then go back into the main chamber.

Surprise Tactics

From the balcony, you can see the Setites in the hatchery and the adjacent corridors. It is possible to attack them from here with ranged disciplines and certain weapons. Have fun disrupting the Setites' defenses!

Take either the left or right door—they both lead into the hatchery. Kill any of the remaining guards in the corridor and enter the hatchery. The vipers are not eager to attack you, so kill them separately as they rest beneath the warming fires. Search behind each nest for treasure that the Setites have offered up to the snakes.

Enter the corridor at the far end of the hatchery and fight your way down the corridor until you enter a room dominated by a white pyramid. Exits lead in all four cardinal directions from this room and six Setites and their snakes guard it.

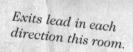

Exits lead in each direction this room.

The exit is straight across the pyramid from where you entered. Each of the other two rooms contains loot and Setite priests. In a corner of the pyramid room, behind a sarcophagus, rests a chainsaw.

Setite Temple 4: Temple of Set

In this small level Lucretia, the leader of the Setites, holds court. This large temple is the center of the Setites' dark worship and, though not heavily defended, is challenging enough.

You enter this level into a room with high ceilings and a central pyramid blocking the way. Fight your way around the sides of the pyramid, dispatching the Setites and vipers that attack you. Take the stairs on the far side of the pyramid down into a hallway lined with columns where two more Setites and their vipers will attempt to deny you entrance to the temple.

Lucretia awaits you in a huge Temple lit by blazing fires.

Lucretia

Type	Ancient Vampire
Description	Lucretia styles herself after the ancient priestesses of the Nile that tended Set's reptilian servants. Her Egyptian garb is very revealing and she loves the shock value it has on opponents.
Health	250
Soak	60/60/60 +60 Soak vs. Fire, Electricity, and Cold
Damage	125 B
Powers	Setite Disciplines at level 3
Weaknesses	No powerful ranged attack.
Tactics	Overwhelm her with your attacks—if she charms any of your coterie, things can go very badly. You should have lots of ammunition, so its possible to use firearms to keep her at a distance and prevent her from attacking you. Use the autofire feature (hold down the ALT key or your third mouse button when attacking) to fire at her continuously.

After fighting Lucretia, you realize that she is not dead and has used ancient magic to place her heart outside her body.

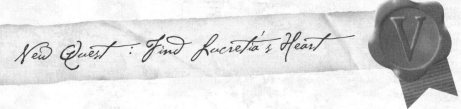

New Quest : Find Lucretia's Heart

Leave the Temple, dealing with any stragglers you may have left, and return to your haven.

From your haven, follow the embankment around the base of the bridge until you come upon the imposing doors of the Tower of London.

Tower of London

Enemies	Wraiths, ghoul spiders, spider swarms
Boss	None
Loot	Monocle of clarity, archaic equipment
Features	Secret room

Overview

In our world, the Tower of London is a brightly-lit tourist attraction holding the treasures of England. In the World of Darkness, it is a cursed place abandoned by mortals, stained with the bloodshed by generations of the British crown. Lucretia has used her powers to place guardians within the building that she intends to use as a second base of operations. The dark and abandoned rooms of the old stonekeep swarm with spiders and the restless dead.

General Tactics

The great danger within the Tower is that sheer numbers overcome your coterie. There are several rooms in the Tower where entire swarms of spiders or wraiths will come at you, and because some of the rooms are very close together, enemies may join in the fight unexpectedly. Modern explosives and flame-throwers can be a great equalizer here, since your enemies have no ranged attacks.

Movement sets off the spider sacs, which launch swarms of tiny vermin, so keep your coterie close together. If you go near one in the middle of a fight, more combatants will join the fray. Either avoid these dangers or set each sac off carefully when you're ready to deal with them.

Navigating the Bloody Tower

The greatest difficulty in navigating the Tower is that there is little light anywhere on the evel. There are no lights within the Tower and flashes of lightning from the storm outside only intermittently light the rooms. Many of the chambers within the Tower are similar, most featuring dark stone walls, cob-webbed corners, and the rusty remnants of instruments of torture. Be careful as you progress through the Tower to avoid becoming hopelessly lost.

Tower of London 1: Traitor's Gate

Spiders have overrun the dark ground floor of the Tower. These bloated monstrosities nest in the ceilings and corners and drop down on hapless intruders. The instruments of medieval torture lie abandoned throughout the level, racks, gibbets and even a guillotine highlight the Tower's past and the reason it got its name.

The wide entrance hall of the Tower disappears into shadowy darkness. Go through the arch to your right and clear two smaller rooms of their resident arachnids. There is some loot to be found amongst the torture equipment as Lucretia has been storing weapons here.

There is loot to be found amongst the torture devices.

Go back into the hallway and walk toward the arched doorway on the left. A spider sac explodes, sending forth a swarm of baby spiders. Kill the vermin, but expect to see more of them. Go through the next two rooms, exterminating the large spiders and either avoiding or carefully activating the pulsating egg sacs.

A large arch opens into a long room with supply crates guarded by spiders. Go through another arch into the room with a grim guillotine and kill the three spiders that guard the weapons there.

Follow the rooms around the edge of the Tower as the tattered curtains blow in the wind.

You must fight spiders in each room, but with care you can isolate the larger spiders from the egg sacs and avoid facing a swarm.

In the last curtained room facing the outside, you can either go straight into a dead end room with some stored supplies or turn right into the heart of the Tower and fight your way up to the stairs.

Tower of London 2: Prison of the Dead

This level is a maze of smaller room and large chambers. Most rooms have two or more exits and they twist back on one another. In the past, this part of the Tower was used as a prison for traitors to the crown and their restless spirits haunt the site of their torment and death.

The stairs twist up into a small room with archways leading in all directions. To the right is a cellblock with instruments of torture in the center of the room. As soon as you enter, the dead will rise up and attack you with their chilling touch.

The dead will rise and attack you.

In a room to one side is another egg sac. To the left is another small room where treasure is guarded by large ghoul spiders. There are several spiders in here and wraiths will emerge from the twisted corpses on the walls.

Leaving this room takes you into a small chamber that the spiders have claimed for their own. Two egg sacs will open and swarm as large spiders drop from above. Doors lead from this room to both the left and the right.

To the right is a second cellblock where wraiths will attack you once again. To the left is a curved room where both spiders and wraiths will attempt to drain your coterie of life. From this room, a small antechamber leads to the stairs up.

Tower of London 3: The Bloody Tower

The stone floors of the lower levels are replaced by wooden floors, which creak and groan beneath your feet. Two spiders attack you as you climb the stairs. Bear right and enter a strange room on the outside of the Tower where four wraiths emerge from pits in the floor.

In an adjacent room, a wraith and two spiders will attack you. The path opens into a larger chamber where more wraiths and spiders guard a secret room. In a corner near the door is a large stone block halfway up the wall. Press this block and part of the ancient stonework slides aside. Inside the hidden chamber is loot and the mystic Monocle of Clarity, stolen by Lucretia from the Tremere!

Go through the arched door into a pillared room where wraiths and spiders attack you. Open the iron door into another cellblock where a final set of wraiths will rise up to torment you. Send them to their rest and climb the stairs.

From one side of this ledge, stairs lead down into a room with treasure guarded by spiders. On the other side of the ledge, stairs lead further to the final level.

Tower of London 4: Heart Chamber

Lucretia has placed her heart in this small room at the top of the Tower. After climbing the stairs, open the iron door and you'll see Lucretia's heart on the table.

Quest fulfilled: Find Lucretia's Heart
New Quest: Return to Lucretia

Pick it up, then climb back down through the Tower to the London streets. Unfortunately, Lucretia has had time to organize a further defense against you. As you leave the Tower, a werewolf bursts from cover and attacks the coterie.

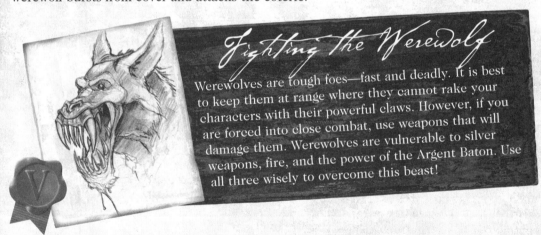

Fighting the Werewolf

Werewolves are tough foes—fast and deadly. It is best to keep them at range where they cannot rake your characters with their powerful claws. However, if you are forced into close combat, use weapons that will damage them. Werewolves are vulnerable to silver weapons, fire, and the power of the Argent Baton. Use all three wisely to overcome this beast!

Stop at your haven to save the game, and then go back to the Setite Brothel.

Temple of Set : Showdown

Overview

The coterie returns to the Temple of Set to face Lucretia for the last time. After entering the Brothel, you will find it deserted. Proceed to the entrance to the Temple and encounter a lone Setite who challenges you and takes you downstairs.

Quest Fulfilled: Return to Lucretia

Lucretia is forced to accede to your demands in exchange for the return of her heart. After she has reclaimed it, she turns on you and transforms into a giant cobra!

Giant Cobra (Lucretia II)

Type	Transformed Vampire
Description	A giant snake, over twelve feet long.
Health	250
Soak	80/80/80 +100 Soak vs. Fire, Electricity, and Cold
Damage	140 A
Powers	Lucretia's cobra form is very fast and its poisonous bite can slay your coterie with ease. It has the powers of Feed, Blood Healing, Mesmerize, and the entire Serpentis discipline at level 3.
Weaknesses	None
Tactics	Lucretia's cobra form is deadly. You must damage it quickly to make sure it does not inflict serious damage on you coterie. Using fire weapons and explosives is very effective—slowing her down enough for you to escape her vicious bite. After dealing sufficient damage to Lucretia, you will be able to attack her amanuensis. He will then drop her heart, which gives you power over her.

Once the Setite has dropped the heart, you can pick it up. Here you get a choice to destroy it and slay Lucretia, or consume it and commit diablerie on her. Committing diablerie carries a humanity penalty, but you can gain one generation, making you more resistant to enemy mind control. Merely slaying Lucretia gets you a small humanity bonus.

New Quest : Board the St. Magdelena

Leave the deserted temple and, instead of proceeding down the steps to your haven, turn left and enter the docks. One ship is docked here—the St. Magdelena. Go up the gangplank to board her.

Quest Fulfilled: Board the St. Magdelena

Inside the ship's hold, a group of Giovanni are fighting the police. The bobbies are slain before you can rush in and destroy the vampires.

Defeat the vampires and the Interpol agent will give you some information.

The dying Interpol agent gives you the information you need to continue, and the ship sails across the Atlantic to the New World and the final battles!

New York

Before beginning the detailed strategy of the New York segment of your adventure, let's briefly discuss each area you'll encounter.

New York Hub

This scene begins with the party standing on the dock. Proceed toward the city through the small tunnel at the beginning of the dock. George Thorn is standing behind some barrels, looking toward a warehouse. Approach him and a conversation will play. Continue into the hub, following the roads. You will come upon a Nosferatu vampire being attacked by three Sabbat. Approach them and, after a short conversation, kill the Sabbat. The vampire is Samuel, who will join your party after a conversation immediately following the fight.

Continue further into the hub. You will see a burning barrel in an alley with a ladder just beside it. Click on the ladder. This takes you to Dev/Null's apartment, which will also serve as your haven for this hub. Walk up and talk to Dev. He will give you a quest to place a transmitter down in the sewers. Exit the apartment. On the street just in front of you there is a partially open manhole. Click on it to enter the Sewers.

Sewers

Near the beginning, you'll come to a tunnel that is blocked by a door. In another room, you'll find two cranks that open that door—turn those and go through this door. Winding your way around, you'll find your way into the second level of the Sewers. Once in here, you'll work your way through more tunnels until you come to a room that looks like an electrical hub or control room. There are two exits from this room (other than the way you came in). One takes you over an electrified metal plated section of the floor and the other takes you to the third rail trap.

There is a small room off this main one with two cranks. Turning one of these cranks deactivates the metal plated floor damage. Deactivate that trap, proceed through here with at least one of your party members, and find another crank in the next room. Turn this one, then finally turn the other crank in the first room. This will deactivate the third rail trap and allow you to proceed into the next level of the Sewers.

In the third level you'll proceed through more tunnels, a 'shroom room, and more goodies. When you reach a large lake, walk toward the skiff that's in front of you and you'll be taken to the opposite bank. From there, proceed into the far-right tunnel and to the Underprince. Defeat him, then go through the door behind him and find the transponder on the wall of the tunnel near the exit ladder. Click on the transponder and exit the Sewers via the ladder.

Giovanni Warehouse

Upon exiting the Sewers, you'll find yourself in uptown New York. Walk around, looking for the Cab. Click on it to get back to the dock area and Dev/Null's place. (This is your means of transportation between the two hub halves.) Return to Dev/Null's apartment and speak with him. After this conversation, the Giovanni Warehouse will be accessible. Exit and proceed back down to the warehouse area, then enter the warehouse (the one that George Thorn was watching).

Upon entering the warehouse, you'll join a gun battle alongside George Thorn. Proceed down to Level 3 of the warehouse and meet Alesandro. Pink will kill him (Shock! Betrayal!), but Wilhem will rejoin the party.

Orsi's End

After exiting the warehouse, head back uptown. Find the Barclay Hotel and enter it. Inside you should see Fred Varney. Talk to him and you will get access to Orsi's penthouse at the hotel. Enter the elevator in the lobby to get to it. At the penthouse you will find Alexandra's palette. Exit the Barclay and walk around to the back of the hotel. There is a door there, leading to some storage rooms. Inside you will find Alexandra. Approach her and, after the conversation, kill the two goons that have appeared in the room. Next, head over to Orsi's factory. Talk to the guards outside of the door and you will be allowed into the factory.

Orsi Factory

Proceed to top of the factory floor. At the very top you will find Orsi. Talk to him, kill him, then head back down to the factory floor. Near the exit from the factory you will find the Triplets. Approach them, speak briefly, then exit the factory. Find the abandoned church (near the exit from the Sewers). Search around for the entrance to the Cathedral of Flesh and enter it.

Cathedral of Flesh

Once in the Cathedral, work your way around the outer hallways to a large iris door. This will take you to the lower level. Wind your way through these hallways and rooms (fairly linear) until you meet Vukodlak. Approach him and you'll have a conversation. Depending on your choice here, the game will either "end" or you'll get sent down to the lowest level of the Cathedral. If you're sent to the lowest level, proceed forward until you come to the "Hall of Memories." Click on each of the pillars in this room to open the iris door. Beyond this doorway, you'll see another pillar and Libussa. Click on Libussa to talk to her and she'll reveal an opening. Take it into the next room and walk past the "hole in the floor." Walking past the hole to the opposite exit takes you back up to the first floor where you will have your final battle with Vukodlak.

Welcome to New York

It is the eve of the millenium when the coterie arrives in New York. Tensions have been building in the World of Darkness far more than the Y2K scare that hit our world. In response to growing unrest, police have set up barricades and checkpoints within the city to prevent any civil disturbance as the clocks strike midnight. The true reason for the growing tensions is not mortal fear over a mere date change, but the psychic emanations from Vukodlak as he rises from slumber. The Big Apple is at the cusp of Armageddon and only you can stop it!

With the docks behind you, walk up the street until you find FBI agent George Thorn crouched behind some pallets, monitoring the Giovanni Warehouse.

Mistaking you for Interpol agents (because of Lily's faked IDs), he shares information with you. Later you will be able to gain access to the warehouse using stolen computer codes, but for now it is sealed.

New Quest : Get the Warehouse Access Codes

Continue up the streets and you'll witness a fight—three other members of his clan are setting upon a lone Nosferatu named Samuel. Kill them and he will join your coterie. Further up the street you will see a fire escape leading into a tenement, the manhole cover entrance to the sewers, a yellow cab, and Winchester's Gun Shop. Visit the gun shop if you need to replenish ammunition or buy more weapons, then climb the ladder into the tenement building.

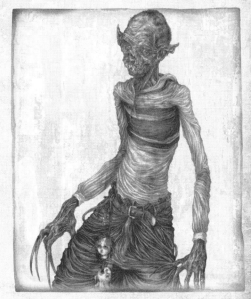

Inside the tenement is Dev/Null's haven, which he will share with you.

Dev is surrounded by his computers.

The lunatic is a brilliant computer hacker and is willing to help you on your quest. Not only can you use his haven, but he also gives you a way to gain entrance into the Giovanni Warehouse, if you first venture into the sewers to attach a transponder to the FBI main computer. He seems very chaotic, but there is sense in his suggestions.

New Quest: Attach Transponder Uplink

Pink's True Identity

Dev says some very strange things to Pink. At the time these seem just to be ramblings, but as it turns out Dev is trying to warn you about Pink's true allegiance—a combination of information surfing and enhanced perceptions allows Dev to pierce "Pink's" disguise. When Dev says "ats a mite stupid name" to Pink, he is referring to Pink's true clan—the Assamites. He is able to rile the assassin enough so that Pink bursts out with "By my beard..." when he is clean-shaven. You receive other clues as to Pink's true nature throughout the game: He is tattooed with Assamite symbols and his jacket has the clan symbol on the back, He also cannot seem to easily stop himself from taking vitae if he ever feeds from another coterie. Unfortunately, Christof has been out of the world for eight centuries and fails to notice any of this.

After entering your haven (the second room in Dev/Null's apartment), leave the tenement and use the manhole cover in the street to gain access to the sewers.

New York Sewers

Enemies	Nosferatu, rats, spiders, alligators
Boss	Underprince
Treasure	Loot
Features	Puzzles

Overview

The upper levels of the Nosferatu lair wind their way between the true sewers and much else of New York's underground. You will find generator substations for the great city's buildings, as well as an unused section of the subway. The Nosferatu have adapted the underground to suit their needs—WWII air-raid shelters are now nests, abandoned foundations have become storage rooms, and the subway is now a playground. There is a beauty in the depths, but it is a tarnished one.

General Tactics

The same tactics you used against the Nosferatu in Josef's Tunnels also apply here. Their invisibility will give them the edge unless you can counteract it with disciplines of your own. Here the problem is compounded by the fact that many of the Nosferatu will use modern firearms against you. Seek to isolate and eliminate lone Nosferatu while keeping the coterie close together to ward off invisible attackers.

Remember that the Nosferatu will often turn invisible as they flee. Do not assume that your foes are dead just because you cannot see them. Many sewer dwellers will flee and then return healed to fight you again. If you pay attention, you can hear the footsteps and cries of Nosferatu that have rendered themselves invisible.

Be careful of the other sewer dwellers—ghoul rats and spiders. Although individually weak, they present a serious threat when they assemble in numbers. Modern weaponry—especially fire-based arms and explosives—will quickly disperse a swarm of these vermin.

Just like their Dark Ages kin, the modern sewer rats are great hoarders. Search their chambers carefully and you will be well rewarded with precious stones and other treasures.

Navigating the Underworld

Because the Nosferatu have sealed off the deeper levels of the sewers, your path is fairly clear. Samuel is able to keep you from descending too far and there are many clear landmarks where the Nosferatu have made their lairs or created traps and art. Side passages and chambers offer opportunities for combat and treasure, but the main path is always straight ahead.

Sewers 1: The Nosferatu Warren

This part of the Nosferatu complex is connected to the vast sewer vents of the docks. Pools of stagnant sewage are common and the bare concrete chambers have been adapted from their original function to serve as lairs for the Sewer Rats.

After climbing down the ladder from the surface, follow the curving tunnel. Rats and a spider guard a side passage that descends into a bottomless pit. Keep going until you hit a larger chamber guarded by three Nosferatu. A large blast door has been sealed shut, so turn left and enter a room overlooking a vast pool of raw sewage. Two Nosferatu and their rat servants guard the wheels that open the blast door.

Turn the wheels to open the blast door.

There's another group of Nosferatu on a platform over the sewage. Kill them to claim the treasures.

Battling Invisible Foes

All except for the eldest Nosferatu must appear when they attack you (those that do not must be revealed through Discipline use or fled). Use these moments of visibility to target them. If you know roughly where a Nosferatu is hiding, use a thrown weapon (for example, a Fragmentation Grenade) and target the floor. If you are correct, the hidden foe will be caught in the explosion.

Go back through the newly opened blast doors, then fight your way past the rats and spiders clustered around the steam vents in the next chamber. In a side room, which was once the flow controls for this section of the sewers, you can find a satchel charge and chainsaw.

Descend the stairs out of the main room and enter a chamber overlooking the stagnant waters of the sewer. Search for loot and then continue onward. The corridor opens into a room that the spiders have claimed as their own—the Nosferatu are tending two large ghoul spiders and many of their children. Exterminate them and claim their treasures, then continue on to a wire frame platform opposite the first sewer pool. Kill the Nosferatu and enter the dark tunnel ahead of you.

Sewers 2: The Subway

This level of the hive connects into abandoned subway systems, left over from the war. The old generators are poorly maintained by their new tenants and are shorting out, making areas of this level dangerous.

The dark tunnel opens into a room guarded by vermin. To one side is a vast chamber, the walls of which are adorned by strange twisted structures of ducts and pipes. This is Nosferatu art.

A steel catwalk leads out over a pool of chemicals—electrical shorts threaten to ignite this volatile mixture and, as you cross, balls of fire explode outward.

Burn Your Enemies

Just like any other flame trap, it is possible to lure your enemies into the danger. To make this experience particularly satisfying, use a mental summoning discipline like Mesmerize or Awe to call one of your enemies into the trap!

Beyond the catwalk, several Nosferatu and their spider allies are stacking trash in dumpsters. As you leave this room, spiders drop on you from the ceiling above. Kill them, then proceed straight ahead into the room containing the Nosferatu art. Here you can find the Tome of Protean.

Leave the art room and continue down the tunnel that opens out onto a platform overlooking a shorting-out electrical generator. To your right is the control room for the generator. If you go down into the pit where the generator rests, two Nosferatu will attempt to kill you. Fight past them and investigate the generator.

Two tunnels extend from the pit. One is blocked close to the generator by an arc of electricity from broken wires on the wall; the other seems safer until you discover a broken subway power conduit grounded in a pool of water. Both of these electrically charged areas are impassable. Use the ungroup commands to separate your coterie and send one character back into the generator's control room, while another character stands by the broken wires. Have the character in the generator control room turn both wheels on the control panel, then have the other character (or characters) run past the broken wires while the circuit is broken.

Battling Alone

Separating a character from the coterie is generally dangerous (because they will be alone in any fights), but can also have advantages. In addition to being able to solve puzzles like this one, a solo character can act as a scout if properly equipped. If the sole character has access to Obfuscate, they will be able to move undetected, scout out enemy positions, and set up ambushes of their own. For example, move the scout past a group of enemies and then attack them from the front. As you attack, hit the Regroup button. The scout will join in the assault, attacking the enemy from behind.

The characters that ran past the wires must now face spiders, rats, and three more Nosferatu as they fight their way into the secondary control room featuring a transformer with a single wheel. Have the characters in each control room turn the wheels together as quickly as possible. If the wheels are turned correctly, the generator will power down and the electrified water will be made safe. Reunite your coterie and go through the pool and out onto the subway tracks.

Here, deep underground, is an abandoned subway station—many Nosferatu guard their prize so you will have to fight your way along the tracks. At the end of the tracks a tunnel leads off or you can climb a pile of broken rubble up onto the platform. If you fight your way past the Nosferatu guarding the crates on the platform, you'll find several treasures and useful items.

After you have investigated the platform, return to the tunnel cut into the side of the subway tunnel and walk into the darkness.

Sewers 3: Deep Tunnels

This area of the Nosferatu lair is deep underground. The Nosferatu practice strange breeding programs here in the depths, so expect to see things only whispered of in the surface world, like gardens of phosphorescent fungi and the fabled albino alligators! Much of this area is in deep darkness and you will need light sources to see clearly. The Nosferatu will use the darkness to their advantage by attacking you from ambush.

Fight your way down the dark tunnel, killing the spiders and rats that dwell there. At the first intersection, turn left and climb through the hole burrowed into the tunnel wall. Steam vents keep the air moist and heavy and two Nosferatu will attack you.

Follow the path out over the depths and then climb the stairs down into the Mushroom Garden of the Nosferatu. Here generations of sewer rats have grown monstrous phosphorescent fungi. Exit the mushroom garden and a small hoard of Nosferatu accompanied by their verminous ghouls will attack you.

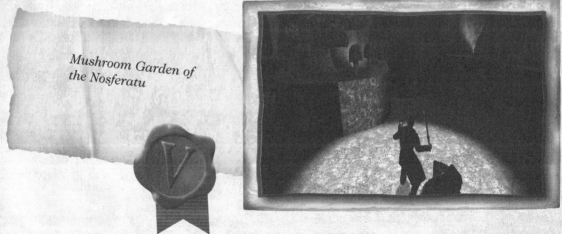

Mushroom Garden of the Nosferatu

The passage curves into a small room where more Nosferatu will fight you. Beyond this room is an area that is almost pitch-black. An ambush has been set, so fight bravely to destroy the defenders.

Battling in the Dark

If you cannot see, you cannot easily fight. Unless you can spare a coterie member to carry a flashlight, you will have to be inventive in creating light. Flame-throwers and explosives will reveal the room in a bright flash, but cannot be used all the time for obvious reasons. If any coterie member has the first power of Thaumaturgy Lure of Flames—Torch—they can create a witchlight to follow them around.

Follow the tunnel away from this room, killing the rats and spiders that dwell here, then take the steel stair down into the lower tunnels. Follow the tunnel as it cuts deep beneath the earth and destroy the Nosferatu and spiders that lurk there. A hole in the underground passage's wall leads to large chamber next to a dark river of the underground. A swarm of rats lives here and they will attack you mercilessly to strip the flesh from your bones. Beyond this rat swarm, the tunnel leads into a huge chamber, which has been filled with water from an underground lake. A creaky skiff provides the only way to cross the lake and it threatens to capsize as pale shapes swim through the water around it.

Use the skiff to cross the underground lake.

On the other side of the lake, albino alligators will drag themselves out of the water and attack you. Give Pink his wish and get some alligator skin boots! Go through the dark tunnel and enter the chambers of the Underprince.

Sewers 4: The Underprince's Chamber

Go down the short tunnel that soon opens into a large chamber. Here the Underprince commands his swarms of rats. Nothing you can say will make him let you past, so you must fight.

The Underprince

Type	Powerful vampire with a swarm of rabid rats.
Description	A bloated, twisted shape in a stained and soiled suit long out of fashion, the Underprince is the undisputed ruler of the downtown portion of the New York sewer system.
Health	100
Soak	40/40/40
Damage	60 A
Powers	Nosferatu level 3-4 (Common, Potence, Animalism, and Obfuscate.)
Weaknesses	Too arrogant to use obfuscate.
Tactics	Ignore the rats—the Underprince can always call on more. Concentrate your attacks on the Underprince himself. Use explosives or fire to clear a path through to him.

After you have killed the Underprince, exit his chamber and proceed through the tunnel to the intersection. Check for any loot and then attach the transponder to large cable junction on the wall. After making contact with Dev over radio, step on the freight elevator and take it to the surface.

Quest Fulfilled: Attach Transponder Uplink

Uptown New York is dominated by the huge façade of the Barclay Hotel. The exit from the sewers is behind the hotel and opposite the New Moon shop. Enter the shop to sell any unnecessary trinkets and barter for mystical items with the owner. After visiting the shop, leave it and go back onto the streets.

If you proceed straight out of the shop, the road that circles the Barclay will split into a side street. Follow it to the Abandoned Church (the location of the Cathedral of Flesh) and Orsi International. Both of these locations are sealed at the moment. Walk around the hotel, taking note of the main entrance and the rear door to the storage room—you will return to both these places later. Just outside the main door of the Barclay is another cab; use it to return to the dock area.

Climb back into Dev's apartment and get the access codes to the Giovanni Warehouse.

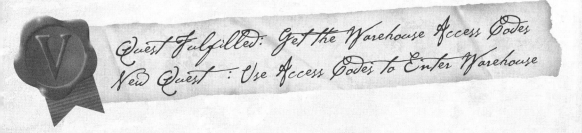

Quest Fulfilled: Get the Warehouse Access Codes
New Quest: Use Access Codes to Enter Warehouse

Leave the apartment and go down the road toward the docks. Near the place where you rescued Samuel, you'll find steps leading up to the side door of the warehouse. Now that you have the codes, you can enter the building.

Quest Fulfilled: Use Access Codes to Enter Warehouse

Giovanni Warehouse

Enemies	Giovanni, wraiths
Boss	Alesandro Giovanni (no fight)
Features	Lots of locked doors and levers to open them
Treasure	Hand of Conrad

Overview

The warehouse is a functional building that's been turned into a fortress by the mobster vampires. The Giovanni deal in weapons and drugs, as well as darker sources of revenue. This insular family of vampires turns to necromancy and other vile practices and you can find evidence of their excesses throughout the warehouse, along with the bound spirits of their many victims. Alesandro's penthouse in the deepest level of the warehouse is lush with stolen treasure.

General Tactics

This is one of the most difficult quests in the game. The Giovanni are coordinated and deadly with heavily modified illegal weapons and use the spirits of the dead as guards and servants. This combination of modern firearms and ancient blasphemy is potent. You will have to use extreme and immediate force to break your way past the many choke points and ambushes.

As spirits, wraiths are resistant to many forms of damage, including firearms. Your best tactic is to use vampiric powers and fire to dispel them. In addition to the many wraiths bound to the factory, many Giovanni can summon personal guardian spirits, so expect to fight more enemies than you initially see.

The Giovanni are a rich clan; consequently, you'll find a great deal of treasure and negotiable currency within the warehouse. You can use this money to buy enhanced weapons for the final stages of the game!

Navigating the Warehouse

The layout of the warehouse is fairly simple, but fighting your way through it is difficult. Many of the doors within the building are locked and can be opened only from control room switches. This means you must frequently search out the controls for a specific door while coming under attack. Also, many of the doors in the smaller rooms open near one another, making it difficult to maneuver through them. This design is intentional on the part of the Giovanni, as they anticipated raids by the authorities or other crime families and designed their warehouse to be as difficult to penetrate as possible.

Giovanni Warehouse 1: Loading Bay

In this area of the warehouse, the Giovanni receive and process their many illegal shipments. Business is booming, so expect to find many storerooms and loading facilities.

The small entrance to the warehouse is unguarded. Go down the dark concrete hallway and confront the first two members of the family. Open the door into an empty stock room and kill the Giovanni there before they can raise the alarm. The door from this room opens up into a loading bay.

Battling the Giovanni

The Giovanni are not inherently tougher than the other vampires you have fought in the game. However, two things make this level difficult: The Giovanni have a lot of money so they can afford an extreme level of military hardware; and, with their powers of Necromancy (Mortis), they can summon the dead to fight at their side. This combination of physical and spiritual strength is very potent and requires great care. Do not get caught in an ambush or crossfire—use your own disciplines to counteract the Giovanni's advantages and show no mercy to the Necromancers.

The doors into the main receiving floor are sealed and several Giovanni attack as you fight your way up the steel stairs to the raised control room. Throw the lever to open the bay doors onto the receiving floor.

Fighting the Giovanni

Go back down the stairs and fight your way onto the floor of the warehouse, past three Giovanni. Tall racks full of packages and crates split this room into narrow aisles. Battle through the aisles to your right and open the door into the shipping room. Kill the Giovanni weighing out cocaine shipments and use the electronic control on the wall to open the door off the receiving floor.

Go down the short corridor, kill the lone Giovanni guard, and open the door at its end. In this stock room, George Thorn is making a desperate last stand against the vampires. Rescue him and continue on with your mission. Open the exit door (right next to the door you came in through) and kill the two Giovanni guarding the elevator (it leads to the lowest levels of the warehouse, but can be activated only from Alesandro's 'penthouse'). Open the door past the elevator into an electronic stock room. Kill the guards, then go through the exit and follow the corridor that leads down, killing the Giovanni that guard the next level.

Giovanni Warehouse 2: Shipping and Packing

Go down the concrete ramp into a small room with double metal doors. Giovanni will try to oppose you as you do so, sniping at you from the cover of crates and barrels.

Explosive Barrels

Several barrels are explosive, containing fuel and other flammable materials. If any of the Giovanni stand next to these barrels, show them the error of their ways by blowing them up!

Open the doors and fight your way past the Giovanni hiding amongst the fuel drums and the ambush point by the crates, then turn right with the corridor. This leads to a balcony overlooking the large shipping room with a freight elevator. Giovanni and their dead servants guard the balcony. Fight your way into the control room.

Go through the door on your right into the control room. Kill the guards and throw the switch, then go down to the shipping room floor. This is a tough fight with several heavily armed Giovanni guarding the room. They are spread out and fire upon you as you approach them. After killing all the vampires, go through the door on the far side.

The corridor switchbacks past fuel drums for the forklift. Blow up the barrels to destroy the Giovanni on guard there, then open the door into a small storeroom, kill the guards, and climb the stairs next to the generator. Open the next door and enter the packing room. You must fight every step of the way past the Giovanni.

Close Combat

The Giovanni have the advantage as they can keep you at a distance—their summoned wraiths can engage you in combat while they overwhelm you with bullets and explosives. In any larger room, you need to use disciplines such as Celerity to close with the Necromancers quickly. In hand-to-hand combat, their military weapons are far less effective.

A conveyor belt divides the packing room. The Giovanni are getting ready to ship currency for laundering and deposit in offshore banks. Kill the vampires managing the machines, then head to your left into the control room. Throw the switch on the wall to open the door beyond the conveyor belt and claim the Tome of Mortis for your own! Go back into the packing room and follow the conveyor belt around, opening both doors and killing the guards.

Follow the corridor past more fuel drums and crates. Open the double metal doors at its end and enter the large storeroom. There are several Giovanni here, as well as the wraiths of prisoners they have tortured to death in the small rooms to the side of the shipping room.

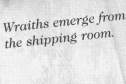

Wraiths emerge from the shipping room.

Fight your way into the second large shipping room, which is as heavily defended as the first, and open the door on the far wall. Go down the concrete ramp, killing the last vampire guards, then open the elevator doors and take it down to the next level.

Giovanni Warehouse 3: Alesandro's Office

Beneath the main body of the warehouse are the rooms of Alesandro Giovanni, the member of the family in charge of New York shipping. He has a richly appointed study and prison cells where he keeps enemies who deserve his special attention.

Follow the concrete ramp that slopes and face the first of Alesandro's guard—three heavily armed Giovanni who are in position to attack you. Continue down and enter the cellblock where two Giovanni will try to bring you down. Just around the corner from the cellblock two more heavily armed guards protect a pair of double doors. Kill them and open the door to Alesandro's study.

Battling in Doorways

If there are enemies on the far side of a door, they will begin firing at you as soon as the door begins to open. Use this to your advantage. As soon as the door begins to open, you can either sprint into the room while they are targeting the door, or pull back from the door. If your enemies are using explosives and fired too soon, their attack may impact the door before it opens fully and they will be caught in the blast.

Alesandro's personal bodyguards are armed with an assault rifle and a grenade launcher. Fight your way into the room and confront the fat mobster. Pink betrays you and destroys Alesandro, revealing himself as an Assamite assassin. He will use his powers to escape as, surprise, Wilhem emerges from the shadows!

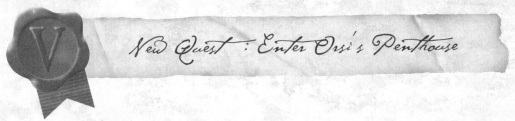

New Quest : Enter Orsi's Penthouse

Search Alesandro's desk and find his Ledger (which confirms Orsi's location) and the Hand of Conrad. Take the elevator outside of Alesandro's study down to the first level of the warehouse (you will emerge close to where you met George Thorn). Make your way to the exit, visit your haven should you need to, then take the cab uptown.

Once the cab drops you off outside the Barclay Hotel, enter it and talk to Fred Varney. Use the elevators in the lobby to go up to the Penthouse. Orsi is obviously preparing to move as the place is in disarray. Much of the furniture is already gone or covered in cloth.

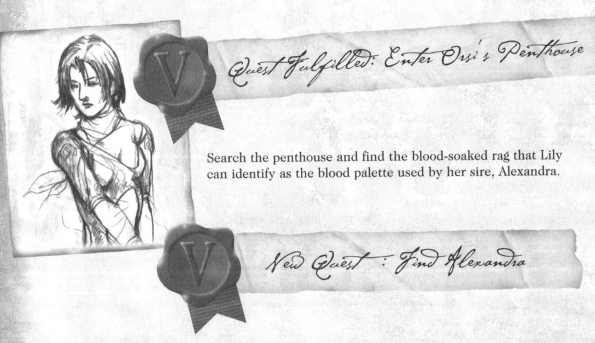

Quest Fulfilled: Enter Orsi's Penthouse

Search the penthouse and find the blood-soaked rag that Lily can identify as the blood palette used by her sire, Alexandra.

New Quest : Find Alexandra

Ride the elevator back down to the Lobby and leave the hotel. Turn right and follow the sidewalk to the back of the building. Here you will find the entrance to the hotel's storage room. Go through the door and confront Lily's sire, Alexandra.

Lily's sire Alexandra

Quest Fulfilled: Find Alexandra
New Quest : Infiltrate Orsi Factory

Vampire-speak

Vampires use the terms sire and childe to refer to the bond between a vampire and the one who created them. There is often a deep psychic bond between the two; this is the reason Christof believes it is Ecaterina that has awakened him from torpor when he meets Wilhem again.

Two of Orsi's goons will try to break up the meeting. Kill them and take the painting of Vukodlak that Alexandra has been working on. With the painting in hand, follow the street past the New Moon Store and the abandoned church to the entrance to Orsi International. The guards will let you in when they see the painting.

Quest Fulfilled: Infiltrate Orsi Factory
New Quest : Find Orsi

Orsi International

Enemies	Ventrue, Tzimisce, szlachta, war ghouls
Boss	Orsi
Features	Twisty layout
Treasure	Loot

Overview

Orsi has done well in the modern age. His medieval fortune has been converted into industrial wealth. He runs a chain of factories in Europe, America, and across the Third World manufacturing weapons, pesticides, and anything else that will make a quick profit. His New York factory is an industrial hell, fortified in preparation for the coming of V-day!

General Tactics

The same general principle applies here as when fighting the Giovanni and Setites. You will be facing heavily armed vampires dedicated to stopping you. Try to separate individuals from the group and destroy them alone; make sure that their superior numbers do not overwhelm you. There is some good treasure in the factory, as Orsi has been using it as a stockpile for when his minions aid Vukodlak's conquest of the antediluvians.

Navigating the Factory

This factory is harder to describe than to play. Basically, there is a core area where you enter and leave. At the center of the floor on the ground level is a large vat of molten steel. Ramps extend up the walls surrounding the vat. At the very top is the control room where Orsi waits. You must go up a ramp, zone into a new level, then exit that level on to a ramp a bit higher than the one you last exited on. Rinse-and-repeat until you reach the top and fight Orsi!

Each level is made complicated by the presence of catwalks over most of the rooms. To move through the factory, you have to clear each room, go up onto the catwalks, then descend into the adjacent room. It's easy to get lost amongst the machinery, so pay attention to the lighting and layout of the individual rooms.

Orsi Factory 4: Central Hub

This is the core of the level. The entrance/exit is opposite the large truck loading doors and there is a vast vat of molten metal in the center of the ground floor. Ramps spiral up above the vat, heading toward the roof and the control room. You will enter and leave this area many times as each separate floor of the factory opens out onto on the ramps—higher up each time. Luckily, nothing guards the ramps so you can rest there.

When you enter the factory, leave the side room and go out onto the factory floor. Walk around the vat of molten steel and climb the concrete ramp up to the first door.

Orsi Factory 1: Power Generators

This level provides the power for the rest of the complex. Most of the rooms contain generators or transformers and the catwalks balance precariously above the electrical grids.

Walk past the generator and climb onto the walkway over the room. If you turn to your left, the walkway leads through and over two rooms guarded by the Ventrue before reconnecting to the main path. Go into those rooms and destroy the defenders descending from the catwalk into each room separately.

Battling the Ventrue

The Blue Bloods are masters of the mental discipline of Dominate and will use it to great advantage. Expect to lose coterie members to the mental powers of your foes. When you lose control over a coterie member, quickly kill the one that has enslaved them to break the control. (A riskier tactic is to throw an explosive at master and thrall; hopefully your foe will be damaged and your friend forced into frenzy, thus turning on the enemy!)

The walkway from the first room reconnects to this catwalk over a live generator. Cross it quickly and descend into the room on the far side. More Ventrue will try to stop you, so kill them and cross the platform over boiling liquid.

Their Tzimisce allies, who have bought war ghouls and szlachta from their secret havens in America, will accompany the Ventrue.

Follow the corridor out of this room through a power substation where you will encounter more of the factory's defenders, then go through the heavy door back to the central ramp. Follow the ramp up and enter the next door.

Orsi Factory 2: Central Processing

The corridors in this level move past the central machinery of the factory. Bodies swing by on conveyor belts to be carried deeper into the factory for processing.

You enter a room guarded by two Ventrue. Kill them both and proceed across the red lit walkway. In the next room, two more Ventrue and a szlachta block your way. Dispatch them and keep going across the green walkway.

If you turn left here down a concrete corridor, you enter a small room full of storage drums where a Ventrue has coaxed a war ghoul into an ambush position. Fight your way down the concrete corridor that exits from this room, killing another war ghoul, and emerge into a large room. You can also reach this room if you turned right at the junction after the green lit walkway. Three Ventrue and a war ghoul guard this room.

117

New York: Orsi International

Deadly Duo

The mix of the physical strength of the war ghouls and the mental power of the Ventrue can be potent indeed. If any of your coterie are mesmerized close to a war ghoul, the beast will use its bone spur to hurl your ally high into the air. Because anyone hit by such an attack is dazed and unable to recover quickly, a war ghoul may repeat this attack until its victim is dead. Rescue your comrades from such a predicament quickly.

Climb the stairs and watch the bodies go by on conveyor belts in one of the processing centers.

After descending to the floor, cross the walkway over more sluices full of chemicals and fight the Tzimisce and their ghoul servants in the next room. Take the metal walkway that leads out of the room.

A pool of chemicals divides the entrance to this room with a similar walkway on the opposite side, upon which stand three Ventrue. You must go around the pool into a sub-control room guarded by Ventrue and szlachta, then head back onto the opposite walkway to reach the exit.

Battling From Afar

You can fire weapons and use disciplines across the pool to affect the Ventrue on the opposite side. Take them out now and they will not be able to reinforce their colleagues in the main room. A very sneaky trick is to use a mental discipline such as Command to turn them on one another.

Follow the walkway on the other side of the pool and go through the door to the central chamber.

Orsi Factory 3: Packing and Storage

This level of the factory is made up of rooms running parallel to each other and connected by steel catwalks. Conveyor belts and other mechanical apparatus are common and break up the rooms.

The room you enter is split in the middle with a conveyor belt and stairs lead up to an overhead walkway. Climb the stairs and descend into the other half of the room. Kill the Tzimisce and the szlachta waiting there and steal their loot. Go back up onto the walkway and move away from the entrance.

Battling Tzimisce

Just like their Dark Ages kin, the modern Tzimisce will use their disciplines to awaken the Beast in your coterie. This can actually be to your advantage, because once a character has frenzied they cannot be mentally controlled. A frenzied character will attack whoever is nearest to them—this includes your enemies, even the one who drove them into rage!

The walkway crosses over some machinery and opens up into another room. Head down to the right and kill the Ventrue guards, then get back onto the walkway and continue to the left. Fight the Tzimisce and the war ghoul on platform and you'll reach a junction.

Go left into a small control room where three Ventrue guard a weapons stash. Go down the other way and fight the Tzimisce and his servants. Climb up onto the catwalk, fighting two more Ventrue, then follow the catwalk around where three more of the clan will try to kill you.

Leave the catwalk and descend to the floor. In a large concrete room, two Ventrue and a pair of reluctant szlachta will attack you. Continue through the next empty room and then fight the four Ventrue guards in the final storeroom. Loot the room carefully and then go around the corner to find the exit onto the central hub

Climb the ramp up to Orsi Penthouse and control room—this is where he oversees the operations of the factory.

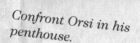

Confront Orsi in his penthouse.

Confront and destroy him, finally claiming vengeance after eight hundred years!

Quest Fulfilled: Find Orsi

After you have killed Orsi, an elevator will take you back to the ground floor of the factory. Run down the ramp and confront the Triplets at the exit. Threaten them so that they reveal Vukodlak's location to you and leave the factory.

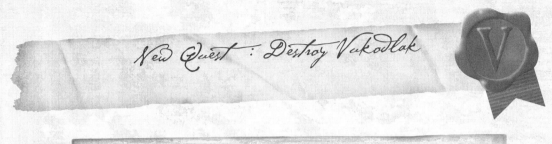

New Quest : Destroy Vukodlak

Humanity Penalties

There is never a penalty for threatening creatures of evil. You face humanity penalties only if you harm innocents.

As you leave the factory and enter the streets of New York, the game launches into a cut-scene. The image switches between the crowded New Year's streets and the clock ticking toward midnight. We see a closed coffin—Vukodlak's tomb! The clock strikes midnight, the crowd goes wild, and the lid of Vukodlak's tomb flies open. We see a long-taloned hand grasping the rim of the tomb! Run through the streets to the church, open the wire gate, and look for the steps leading down into the darkness.

Vukodlak's hand grasps the rim of the tomb.

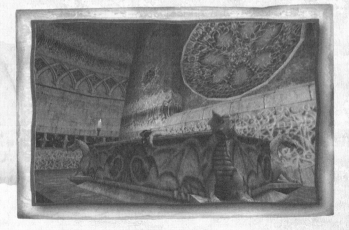

The Cathedral of Flesh

Enemies	Tzimisce, Vozhd, szlachta, war ghoul, demon hounds, etc.
Boss	Vuklodak, Zulo
Treasure	Some loot and a few weapons

Overview

The Cathedral of Flesh is the masterpiece of Tzimisce evil. Crafted from the living bodies of hundreds, if not thousands, of mortals and vampires alike it is a living structure designed to amplify the power of the Voivode. The desecrated church looks almost normal with only a few strange extrusions of flesh in dark corners, but as you progress the true horror becomes apparent. The corridors and chambers of the Cathedral have been crafted from human flesh and bone. Rivers of bile and other less savory fluids flow beneath the veinous corridors and vast ribcages support the ceiling. Human faces, twisted in agony, swim through the pestilential walls of this blasphemous place and here and there you can see dying mortals gradually being absorbed into the structure.

General Tactics

All the monsters you face in the Cathedral—war ghouls, szlachta, and rats—have been enhanced by the presence of Vukodlak. Do not automatically dismiss them as simple enemies, because they are stronger and faster than before. None of them possesses ranged attacks, however, so you can mow them down with automatic weapons fire.

The Vozhd is a very dangerous opponent capable of killing your coterie in a few powerful blows and vicious bites. Use your disciplines to distract or destroy this beast before it can get close enough to fight you.

The Tzimisce in the Cathedral are all elders of the clan who have come to America following the Voivode's dream. Expect no mercy from them—they have cast off all human concerns. As powerful vampires, they prove difficult to kill, so attack them constantly to make sure that they have no chance to heal.

Navigating the Cathedral

For all of its horror, the Cathedral is very basic in design. The desecrated church on its uppermost level is based around a series of rooms encircling the central chancel. The Cathedral itself follows the design of human flesh. Enter through the path and proceed straight down into the gullet!

Cathedral of Flesh 1: Desecrated Church

The Voivode has corrupted this old stone church. It's original beauty lies in ruins and the statues and furnishings have been twisted into a mockery of Christian worship.

You enter into the main chancel of the church—a large pillared room empty of enemies. There are two doorways leading from here; take the one at the front of the church where the altar should be. A balcony looks out over the growing mounds of flesh that are pushing up from below and you can see a sealed sphincter door. Kill the war ghoul and go through the passage into a side shrine. A second war ghoul and its szlachta cousin attack you here—the area's holy faith has long since been defiled. Continue to follow the passage around the outside of the chancel into a room with a broken prayer booth. Three Tzimisce claim this room and will attack you as you enter. As you continue on, you break into a cavernous room that has been modified to hold a Vozhd. Kill this monstrous beast as quickly as you can. Once the creature is dead, the sphincter into the lower Cathedral opens.

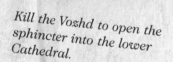
Kill the Vozhd to open the sphincter into the lower Cathedral.

Battling the Vozhd

The Vozhd is large enough that it can easily pick up one of your coterie and chew on them like a child with a lollipop. Do not let it get close enough to do this! Use ranged weapons and powers to take it down and limit its attacks by staying in the corners and doorways of the room where it cannot easily reach you.

Enter a small room held by two war ghouls and a Tzimisce. An arched exit connects this room back to the main body of the church; ignore it and press onward into another side chapel. The Tzimisce and their servants have corrupted this place and set up their own worship here. Kill the guardians and lay claim to the Tome of Animalism.

As you leave this room, the passage slopes downward and soft flesh replaces stone. Cross the bleeding mass and enter into the Cathedral.

Cathedral of Flesh 2: Cathedral of Flesh

This level is made from the sacrificed flesh and bones of countless victims. The walls pulsate and scream, bile flows beneath the bone walkways, and strange sounds can be heard echoing throughout its blasphemous halls.

Walk along the bone and blood pathway, slaying the war ghoul that shambles toward you. The walkway widens into a chamber where some of the old stonework is still visible. A war ghoul and szlachta attack you. If you go down the side passage to the left, you can fight a group of Tzimisce, war ghouls, and szlachta in a grotesque chamber with fibrous flesh hanging for the ceiling.

Keep going down the passage and, as it turns, fight the demon hounds Vukodlak has summoned to guard himself. The passage widens again into a bone platform over the liquid pits and you will face a tough fight against three war ghouls.

The fleshy Cathedral

Battling War Ghouls

War ghouls love to attack as a group. Together they can use their bone spurs to continuously juggle a character, never letting them get their bearings. To prevent this from happening, keep your coterie together so that you can take down groups of these monsters more easily.

Beyond them is a huge room where a second Vozhd dwells, lording over demon hounds and szlachta. Destroy these monsters and head down the bloody passage into the Chamber of the Voivode. Vukodlak is fully awake and ready to confront you. He will suffer no further opposition in his quest for godhood.

Once you have inflicted sufficient damage on the Voivode, he tires of the fight and opens a pit from the very floor of the cathedral, hurling you into its bowels.

When you face Vukodlak, you may be given a choice as to how you respond to the monster, depending on your Humanity trait. If you have a high humanity, your only thought will be to save Anezka and destroy Vukodlak and you will receive no choice. If your humanity is below 50, however, you can choose to submit to the Fiend or to drink his heart's blood. These choices will lead to the alternate endings to the game.

Cathedral of Flesh 3: Bowels of the Cathedral

If you choose to defy the Voivode, he unceremoniously dumps you into the bowels of the Cathedral to be consumed. The chambers at the base of the Cathedral are twisted combinations of flesh and stone.

From the large starting chamber ribbed with bones and offal, fight your way into the corridor. War ghouls, demon hounds, and szlachta that have been condemned by their master are eager to rise in the Cathedral's hierarchy and will attempt to tear you apart. Follow the corridor over a river of bodily fluids until it comes to a dead end closed off by a sphincter. In alcoves lining the walls are what seem to be the faces of Anezka! Click on each of these faces in turn to have her story revealed to you. This is the wall of memory where Anezka has preserved her very self from defilement. Once you have heard this sad tale, the sphincter opens.

Walk into the ventricle of the Cathedral and visit Libussa. She has despaired and is willing to help you escape. Trust her and she will open the way out for you. Walk into the aorta chamber and take the weapons, then proceed through the veinous corridor back to the surface.

After all this drama, the coterie is in the desecrated church once more. Proceed into the main chancel of the church and meet Vukodlak! He transforms into his battle-form—the Zulo!

The final fight is against Vukodlak in Zulo form.

124

Vukodlak in Zulo Form

Type	Ancient Vampire in battle-form, a horror out of the past.
Description	With his mastery of Koldunic sorcery complete, Vukodlak can call on all the power of the Tzimisce to transform himself into their ancient battle-form. Flaunting a vast, long-limbed body with wings, a barbed tail, and a head close to the terrible lizards of a bygone age, the Zulo form is an expression of his ultimate mastery over the flesh and rejection of the human form!
Health	550
Soak	100/100/100 +100 Soak vs. Fire, Electricity, and Cold
Damage	140 B
Powers	The Zulo form is the ancient battle-form of the Voivode. A nightmare killing machine, Vuklodak maintains his mind and can use his terrible sorcery in this form. (Common, Animalism, Blood Magic, and Call Lightning at 4 or 5!)
Weaknesses	None
Tactics	This is the last stand for Christof's soul—and the fate of humanity. Use everything you have immediately. Should Vuklodak win, the eternal night will fall.

This is the final fight. If victorious, we launch into the happy ending video, and then the credits roll.

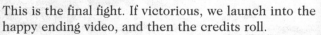

The Endgame

How can Christof possibly win? If you do beat Vukodlak, you may wonder how it is possible that a relatively young vampire like Christof could beat an ancient monster like Vukodlak. Here are some possibilities for you to muse over:

Christof is inspired by his love for Anezka and his human spirit. This gives him the edge over the static and corrupt Tzimisce.

Christof is destiny's chosen agent to stop Vukodlak. As such, he is the hero fated to bring down this ancient evil.

The ways of the Jyhad are subtle and complicated. Those who pay attention to such things whisper that something older than Vukodlak makes its lair beneath New York City. Perhaps this being wished Vukodlak to be bought low and arranged for a hero to be successful. Perhaps you have been subtly manipulated all along…

Characters

Our Heroes

Christof Romuald

Clan: Brujah

A young Frenchman, Christof has seen too much slaughter and his eyes are weary. An acclaimed warrior with the holy order of the Swordbrethren, he has seen more combat than men twice his age and each death on the battlefield has stripped away a little more of his soul. Before he fell in the battle of Moravia, his heart was empty and his faith dead.

Nursed back to health by Sister Anezka, her gentle care rekindled feelings he had forgotten in the blood-rage of battle. As he falls to the curse of Caine and she begins her quest to save him from the darkness, no one knows if their story will be one of redemption or damnation.

Destiny

Christof's destiny is in your hands. You will decide if he falters and falls or raises himself and Anezka up.

Serena

Clan: Cappadocian

As pale as death and twice as beautiful, Serena is a true childe of Cappadocius. The mysteries of eternity are a source of endless fascination to her and she often mocks the mayfly, brief lives of mortals around her. This *belle dame sans merci* recognizes both the darkness in Christof's soul and his potential for salvation. She is drawn to him just as much as she turns away from him into the eternal night she calls home.

Destiny

The Clan of Death is ushered into the mysteries of the afterlife by the rising Giovanni. No Cappadocian survives the centuries-long purge and Serena is surely lost in some long-forgotten battle against the Italian necromancers.

Wilhem Streicher

Clan: Brujah

Wilhem is reticent about his background, but it is known that, although he was a soldier, he was never a knight. Other Brujah whisper he was a brigand or footpad, but never to his face. Wilhem has found purpose in battle. Here the philosophical quandaries of damned existence are resolved into the eternal moment of battle. Hailing from Germany, this pragmatic monster finds peace in war, and contentment in damnation.

Destiny

Centuries of war and the growing threat of the Final Nights causes Wilhem to forsake both the path of *Humanitas* and the Promethean ideal.

Erik McDonough

Clan: Gangrel

Hailing from the Celtic wilds of the north, this massive man was embraced over two centuries before he meets Christof. A barbarian who rejects civilization and the weak vampires he finds there, Erik holds to an ancient path of honor and commitment that would shame the most chivalrous knight. Like many of his clan, Erik prefers the untamed wilderness and the challenges that can be found there to the viper's nest of the cities.

Destiny

Erik falls to his enemies, the Tremere, facing Etrius himself. The ancient Gangrel never survives to see the modern nights.

Pink

Clan: Brujah

Pink is an enigma. Although he appears to be a raging Brujah, a stereotype borne out by his outrageous punk fashions and street slang, there is something odd about him. The vampires of London are not sure what to make of this rebel hero and generally avoid his company. Pink couldn't be happier about this, scoring their fear and relishing the stir he is making.

Those who look closely at him come away disturbed. His aura is broken by dark lines—a sign he has fed on the heart's blood of other vampires—his tattoos seem foreign, different from the tribal tats adopted by other young Brujah, and every now and again he refers to events no modern Brujah could have seen.

Is he just a modern jester using cockney slang and a punk attitude to rile the elders or is he something darker... Only time will tell.

Destiny

Pink escapes the final confrontation in New York, revealing his true self to the world. Who knows if the master assassin will cross swords with Christof again?

Lily

Clan: Toreador

Lily is a young vampire. An aspiring singer, she was bought into the darkness for her beauty and her voice. On her grand tour (a Toreador tradition in which the young of the clan travel the great cities of the world), she was seduced and blood bound to the Setite, Lucretia. When we first meet her, she has been a slave for over a year and is desperate to escape.

Destiny

Should Lily survive the final battle with Vukodlak, she will be able to reunite with her beloved sire, Alexandra, and continue her career as an immortal chanteuse.

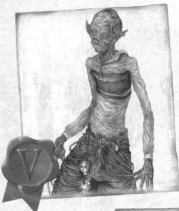

Samuel

Clan: Nosferatu

The tunnels beneath New York have been the site of an unseen war for human generations. The Nosferatu creeps of the Sabbat have been cementing their sect's stronghold on the city from below and they will tolerate no resistance to their plans. Samuel disagrees with his clan-mates and seeks independence, tending more toward the Camarilla's Masquerade than the Sabbat's crusade.

Destiny

Should he survive, Samuel will be instrumental in the Camarilla's war to re-take New York; helping the Nosferatu justicar, Cock Robin, to lead his attack through the sewers.

Allies and Enemies

Sister Anezka

A young nun with a purity of faith that can make monsters weep, Anezka is an enigma. Her hope protects her from the Tzimisce revenants, the Tremere warlocks, and all other foes until she meets the Voivode Vukodlak, who drags her down into darkness.

For eight centuries she serves the monster as a blood-bound ghoul slave, yet still her spirit is not broken. Across the centuries, she summons her champion to fight for her and the world on the cusp of the millennium.

Archbishop Geza

Archbishop Geza is a corrupt old man who has lost the last vestiges of the faith that bought him into the church. Geza delights in the ecclesiastical trials and crusades that are occurring as they bring more land and more wealth into the church. He meets his fate during Devil's Night, dying of apoplexy as he attempts to flee with his chests of treasure.

Ecaterina the Wise

A native of Prague, Ecaterina always resisted the role others assigned to her. She would not accept the narrow life of a medieval matron and struck out on her own. This independence drew a Brujah elder to embrace her and turn her force of will to the Promethean cause. Her face is scarred from wounds received when she was raped just before her embrace. As the centuries pass, Ecaterian becomes more independent and fierce of spirit, eventually becoming a bishop for the Sabbat in New York.

Cosmas

An ancient soldier, Cosmas remembers time long gone when Prague was a frontier outpost for the legions of Rome. This old soldier finds no room for social niceties or politics, preferring action to words. He falls on Devil's Night as the war between Tremere and Tzimisce, mortal and immortal surges across Prague

Garinol Cappadocius, Abbot of Petrin Hill Monastery

Garinol has adapted well to Christianity, adopting the guise of a humble abbot. This is merely a disguise, for the master of death magic is a powerful vampire and a follower of the Cainite Heresy. His one mistake was in the embrace of his 'son' Mercurio. He disappears when his ship sinks while attempting to flee to the New World.

Prince Rudolf Brandl

A puppet prince, Brandl is desperate to shore up his faltering reign. His power is constricted by the ancient Tzimisce Voivodes who control the Premsyl dynasty on one side and the growing menace of the Tremere warlocks on the other. A sycophantic autocrat, his reign ends when he orders Josef to open the ghetto to his cronies so they may feed there. That night, Josef enters the prince's chambers and slays him before he can rise for the evening.

Josef Zvi

The defender of the Ghetto of Prague, Josef was born the son of rabbi and reborn into darkness as a defender of his people. For all his monstrous appearance, he continues to care deeply for his people throughout the centuries, eventually deposing Prince Brandl and becoming the new prince when the Ventrue's abuses become too great. Josef endures the centuries until he falls before Nazi troops sometime in the late 1930s.

Illig

An ancient Nosferatu loremaster who seeks to understand the mysteries of Caine, Illig guards the labyrinth beneath Prague. He is in awe of the master craftmason Zelios and often has to be fed by his clan-mates, lest he slip into torpor in meditation over the Labyrinth.

King Vaclav

A great lord and founder of the Premsyl dynasty, Vaclav was buried with full honors beneath the greatest cathedral in Prague. Mortal scholars never recorded what darkness disturbs his rest, though legends have it that his ghost walks to this very day.

Ardan of Golden Lane

Ardan sees immortality as a prize that must be seized with both hands. He seeks to impress the elders of his clan so that he might rise to ever-greater power, building a chantry in Prague is but one step in that plan. Although it appears that he dies at the hands of Christof, a Tremere called Ardan Lane oversees the work of the warlocks in Prague and the surrounding countryside until the end of the Twentieth Century.

Orvus

Orvus has seen the world change since he was awakened to the magic. The ancient and majestic Order of Hermes has split. As one house has rebelled and become a clan of vampires, magic fades like a dream and the proud hopes of a mythic age seem distant to him. Still he maintains a chantry in Vienna, hoping that the riddles of this age can be solved so that a new one can begin. In the coming century, Orvus flees this world for the Horizon and disappears from mortal history.

Count Orsi

Orsi is an ambitious young Ventrue. He has come to Vienna to build a fortune that will last centuries and does not care that he deals in human misery. He survives the centuries growing fat and lazy, diversifying his interests from slaves to opium and tea in the Eighteenth Century, and finally to modern armaments in the Twentieth. He survives all the upsets of Cainite history until he meets Christof once more after eight hundred years. Their reunion is brief.

The Triplets—Kazi, Teta, & Zil

Three beautiful Cainites, the 'daughters' of Count Orsi, the Triplets are Orsi's most effective agents. Deadly intriguers, it seems at times as if they merely tolerate their 'father' and have their own deep agenda. It is not known what happens to them after Vukodlak's awakening, but careful research shows that many of Orsi's assets were liquidated quickly in the early days of January 2000 and no one knows where the money went…

Etrius

How many years does a mortal have to learn wisdom? How many more years does a wizard have? How many centuries does it take a vampire to regret its embrace? These are the questions that haunt Etrius as he dutifully serves his master, Tremere, down the endless centuries. Leading the clan from strength to strength, Etrius dreams of a creature with three eyes and wonders if it was all a mistake.

Vukodlak

Self-proclaimed Voivode of Voivodes, this ancient monster defies his own clan and all that stand before him, searching for the secrets of true immortality and eternal dominion over the world. In a lesser being such thoughts would be called madness, but in Vukodlak they are a cold sanity.

Libussa

The broken shell of one of Vukodlak's conquests, Libussa is merely a mouth for the words the Voivode dreams. Her life is merely an eternity of torment and defilement with no gleam of hope other than death.

Father Leo Allatius

Leo Allatius wrote a famous book on witch-hunting in the Seventeenth Century, but who could have dreamed that same man would walk the earth for over two centuries. A fanatical vampire hunter, Father Allatius drinks the blood of his victims to survive the centuries-long crusade that he hopes will bring a New Jerusalem into being on the ashes of the old world.

Sumner Montague

An old daguerreotype shows this portly gentleman looking out over the Thames at the turn of the last century. A shopkeeper, antiquarian, and minor celebrity in the London club scene, Sumner lives quietly above his little shop, hoarding his power like a miser hoards gold.

Lucretia

The Followers of Set do not see vampirism as a curse, but rather as the blessing of their dark god, Set. Lucretia has been the high priestess of this ancient legend for many years, taking over an abandoned theatre and turning it into a brothel and nightclub during the Egyptian craze of the Twenties. The neighborhood has seen better days, but the slow corruption of London continues.

Dev/Null

The Malkavians see the world differently from the rest of us. Some call them mad, others say that they see too much. Hunched before his bank of monitors, his servers, and system tools, Dev sees far more than one might expect. As he watches the tides of the sea of data, he sees infinity and it speaks to him.

George Thorn

Special Agent Thorn is a man to be reckoned with. One of the youngest agents ever to achieve Special Agent status, he pursues a war on crime with all the means at his disposal. Over the years, there have always been odd cases—bodies disappearing from morgues, exsanguinations, killers that no one saw—but he has always written off the spooky explanations. Now as he approaches the fringes of a criminal empire run by the Giovanni family, all that is about to change. The truth is out there, Special Agent George Thorn.

The Underprince

There has always been filth beneath the cities, and there have always been things that swim in that filth. The self-proclaimed Underprince is one of those things. Rising amongst the Sabbat through inspired viciousness and sheer cruelty, he rules because no one dares deny him. His death in 1999 helps pave the way for the Camarilla assault on the sewers and the re-taking of New York.

Alesandro Giovanni

If he weren't so good with numbers, Alesandro would be an embarrassment to the family. The Italian mobster schtick is a stereotype most Giovanni abhor, but Alesandro loves it. His collection of Mafia films, 'family pictures' he calls them, is rivaled only by his extensive library of pornography. Still when business is this good—guns to fuel wars to protect the drug fields to buy more guns—a little excess can be overlooked.

Bestiary

You will meet a host of enemies on your quest to find redemption. Many will be humans or vampires, but there are other strange things in the World of Darkness that you will encounter.

All creatures in the game share the same attributes and traits as your characters; their combat abilities are calculated identically and any disciplines they may use have the same effects and costs.

Special Attacks

There are a few special attacks that require a little more explanation.

Poison

The creature's attack has a chance of introducing poison into your body on a critical hit. If you are poisoned, your health will drop and your frenzy level will rise until you can administer an antidote or the poison wears off. Vampiric Blood Healing can remove the damage inflicted by poison, but will not cure it; the only way to do that is with an Antidote.

Disease

The creature's attack has a chance of introducing a disease into your body on a critical hit. If you are diseased, your health will drop and your frenzy level will rise until you can administer a Vaccine or the disease wears off. Vampiric Blood Healing can remove the damage inflicted by disease, but will not cure it; the only way to do that is with a Vaccine. The damage from disease is somewhat less than that inflicted by poison, but its effects take longer to wear off.

Secondary Attacks

Any actor in the game can use a secondary attack just like your character. For most monsters, this attack does double damage, but for some there are other effects, too. For example, huge monsters, such as the Vozhd and War Ghouls, can pick up man-sized targets and hurl them into the air. The victim of such an overwhelming attack is dazed and confused for a short period of time, assuming they survive the assault.

139

Bestiary Stats & Strategy

This bestiary is broken down into categories—Critters; Humanoid Opponents; Spirits, Bygones, & Other Oddities; Lawmen; Summoned Creatures; Vampires; Minor Bosses; and Major Bosses.

Damage and Soak

Damage given is the base damage—any enemy with powers can upgrade their damage through discipline use. The special (secondary) attack will do even more damage!

The soak totals reflect the armor rating of the monster, not their stamina. All characters get to use their stamina to soak damage according to certain rules.

Critters

Critters include animals and other things that creep and crawl!

Ghoul Rat

Type	Vermin (Ghoul)
Health	20
Soak	0/0/0
Damage	10 B
Special Attacks	Can cause disease.
Description	Grown to the size of dogs, these monsters terrorize the weak.
Tactics	Take out the rats one at a time, being careful not to get surrounded—a pack of these beasts can bring down an armored knight.

Ghoul Rat Leader

Type	Vermin (Ghoul)
Health	30
Soak	0/0/0
Damage	30 B
Special Attacks	Can cause disease.
Description	These albino monsters dominate the rat packs.
Tactics	A couple of good sword blows will dispatch these vermin.

Szlachta

Type	Twisted Servant (Ghoul)
Health	80
Soak	0/0/0
Damage	20 B
Special Attacks	Can cause disease. As a ghoul, can use Blood Healing and Potence.
Description	The victims of Tzimisce experimentation, the szlachta are shambling monsters made of the flesh of many victims.
Tactics	You can easily outrun these beasts should you need to. If encountered singly, they present little challenge, but in groups they may be dangerous.

Szlachta Boss

Type	Tough Servant (Ghoul)
Health	90
Soak	0/0/0
Damage	50 B
Special Attacks	Can cause disease. As a ghoul, can use Blood Healing and Potence.
Description	More hideous than its smaller cousins, the szlachta boss uses a bone club and has tattoos that mark its place in the Tzimisce hierarchy. (In the modern day you may encounter szlachta wielding baseball bats!)
Tactics	Be more careful around these creatures than the smaller szlachta. Use your secondary attack (SHIFT + left-click) to take them down faster.

War Ghoul

Type	Tough Servant (Ghoul)
Health	100-150
Soak	0/0/0
Damage	70 B
Special Attacks	Can cause disease. As a powerful ghoul, it can use Blood Heal, Fortitude, and Potence.
Description	A twisted monstrosity made out of fleshcrafted victims. It can attack with a wicked bone spur that has been grown out of its arm.
Tactics	War Ghouls are dangerous opponents. Their bulk makes them hard to kill and their bone spur is capable of dealing severe damage. When they prepare to make this attack (you will see them drawing back their arm), dodge out of the way to avoid it.

Wolf

Type	Animal
Health	40
Soak	0/0/0
Damage	25 A
Special Attacks	None
Description	The ancient timber wolves of Europe, these beasts hunt in packs and are terrors in winter when food becomes scarce. The Tzimisce keep them as pets.
Tactics	Wolves are scarcely a threat to you. If you have developed the Animalism Discipline, you can seize control of their minds and turn them on their masters. Be careful—what you think is a wolf may in fact be a shape-shifted vampire using the Protean discipline, Form of the Wolf!

Hopper

Type	Homunculi
Health	40
Soak	0/0/0
Damage	20–30 A
Special Attacks	A hopper can cling to its victims like a lamprey, sucking the vitality from them.
Description	The product of alchemical experimentation, these critters are servants and watchdogs for the Tremere. Individually weak, they can be deadly in a swarm.
Tactics	Do not let a swarm cling to you or they will strip you to the bone like piranhas. Strike them as they come at you and never let one get behind you!

Ghoul Spider

Type	Arachnid Ghoul
Health	120
Soak	50/0/0
Damage	85 A
Special Attacks	Poison
Description	Vast and bloated, these nightmarish creatures drop from the ceilings on unwary foes.
Tactics	You can see their shadows before they drop, so direct your attacks on them as they descend to get rid of them.

Baby Spiders

Type	Arachnid Ghoul
Health	60
Soak	20/0/0
Damage	30 L
Special Attacks	Poison
Description	Vast swarms of small spiders that burst forth from egg sacs.
Tactics	Like any other swarm, you must break it up to stand a chance. An explosive weapon will halt several of these arachnids in their tracks.

Ghoul Alligators

Type	Animal (Ghoul)
Health	200
Soak	30/30/30
Damage	110 A
Special Attacks	With the Nosferatu blood in their system, Ghoul Alligators may use the Disciplines of Blood Healing, Potence, and Fortitude
Description	The urban legends are true—alligators do live in the sewers of New York! This particular breed has grown fat in the spawning pools of the Nosferatu.
Tactics	The alligators' bite will do a tremendous amount of damage. Use ranged attacks to keep them at a distance and do not let them get close enough to bite you. They can toss a fully grown adult some distance if they close their jaws fully on a target!

Viper

Type	Animal
Health	20
Soak	0/0/0
Damage	6
Special Attacks	Poison
Description	Slithering snakes, some natural others summoned through Setite magic.
Tactics	Kill them quickly—their poison can affect even the children of Caine.

Humanoid Opponents

Ghoul

Type	Ghoul
Health	40-60
Soak	0/0/0
Damage	25–60 L (by weapon)
Special Attacks	Blood Healing and Potence
Description	Ghouls are humans who have voluntarily ingested vampire blood to gain a measure of power. Specific ghouls (like the Lasombra ghouls you meet in Stephansdom) are tougher, but not significantly so.
Tactics	Tougher than any human, these servants pale in comparison to their vampiric masters. Overall, they should present little challenge to your coterie.

Revenant

Type	Ghoul
Health	60-100
Soak	0/0/0
Damage	25–60 L (by weapon)
Special Attacks	Blood Healing and Potence
Description	Revenants are those ghouls who were born to the condition after centuries of selective breeding. They are more powerful than regular ghouls and, hence, look down on them.
Tactics	Once again, these foes are almost human and should not delay you for too long.

Teutonic Knights

Type	Human
Health	70
Soak	60/80/30
Damage	60–90 B or L (by weapon type)
Special Attacks	None
Description	Heavily armored knights on a crusading mission across Eastern Europe, these are amongst the toughest human foes you will face.
Tactics	The knights have a lot of physical power, but no magical powers or resistance. Use disciplines to overwhelm them. The knights are at a severe disadvantage because of their heavy armor—it blocks their perceptions. As such, it is very easy to sneak up on them or dispatch a lone knight without alerting his comrades.

Society of Leopold Worker

Type	Human
Health	70
Soak	45/45/25
Damage	20–60 or special (by weapon)
Special Attacks	Given the present danger of Kindred assault, the workers carry holy water and stakes, as well as mundane weapons. The fanatics of the Society of Leopold also have access to the powers of True Sight and True Faith.
Description	The scientists and researchers of the Society dress in functional blue lab coats.
Tactics	The workers are not a threat unless they are in a group. The biggest danger comes from the Holy Water some of them will throw at you—it damages vampires, but has no effect on the other humans. Their power of Faith can damage you if you approach them, so it's best to kill them at range using either your mental disciplines to negate their threat or simply ranged modern weapons.

Society of Leopold Soldier

Type	Human
Health	100
Soak	80/80/40
Damage	50–80 or special (by weapon)
Special Attacks	These soldiers use modern firearms, including Incinerators and Assault Rifles. They also have access to the powers of True Sight and True Faith.
Description	The well-trained soldiers of the Society dress in fascist uniforms and stand ready to defend humanity against the omnipresent threat of the supernatural.
Tactics	Because they are well armed, it is best to use your disciplines to scatter the soldiers—cloud their minds or disappear to avoid their attacks. Because of their faith, they not only stand a chance of seeing should you become invisible, but can also damage you if you approach them closely. This combination of modern weapons and fanaticism can be quite deadly, so use your disciplines to undo their ambushes and turn them upon each other.

Spirits, Bygones, & Other Oddities

These creatures are all things that have hidden or disappeared from the mortal world. They are the beasts of legend that still creep and crawl in dark places. Bygones were rare even in the Dark Ages, and by the Modern Nights they are thought to be all but gone from the world.

Wraith

Type	Spirit
Health	120
Soak	Immune/60/60, Immune to Cold and Electricity
Damage	55 Cold
Special Attacks	None
Description	The tormented damned appear as shadowy figures in our world. They bear a tremendous hatred for the living and vampires alike.
Tactics	As you can see from their soak total, it is difficult to damage a Wraith. Use Fire and Aggravated damage (Feral Claws for example) to dispel them. On a critical hit even mundane weapons may damage them, but you should not rely on this to happen.

Werewolf

Type	Werewolf
Health	150
Soak	0/0/0
Damage	100 A
Special Attacks	None
Description	Known as Lupines by vampires, these beasts seek to tear down both human civilization and its vampire overlords. Huge and bestial, they are relics of a time long gone.
Tactics	Werewolves are deadly fighters—fast and strong. Avoid them when you can, only fight if you must. Because of the great damage they inflict with their claws and teeth, you must kill them quickly to survive. Werewolves are vulnerable to silver, so equip yourself with a silvered weapon if you face them.

Vozhd

Type	Ghoul
Health	250
Soak	30/30/30; +30 Soak against Fire, Electricity, and Cold
Damage	160 A
Special Attacks	A Vozhd can pick up a full-grown man and chew on his head. Nasty!
Description	A vast conglomeration of the flesh of dozens of victims, the Vozhd is the ultimate monstrosity and the ideal weapon in the Tzimisce bestiary.
Tactics	You cannot allow a Vozhd to engage you in physical combat, as it will surely win. Hurt it from range or use disciplines to evade it.

Zombu/Corpse Minion

Type	Undead
Health	80
Soak	0/0/0
Damage	35 B
Special Attacks	None
Description	Raised from the dead by necromancy, these shambling nightmares follow the commands of their vampire masters.
Tactics	They are very slow moving so it is easy to retreat from battle and attack them with ranged weapons or separate them from the group.

Dark Hunter

Type	Shadow
Health	50
Soak	Immune/Immune/0
Damage	70 A
Special Attacks	None
Description	The shadows of elder Lasombra vampires given an independent existence, these strange phantasms exist somewhere between the real world and the world of eternal night, from which they draw their power.
Tactics	Like Wraiths, these beings are hard to kill. Use Aggravated damage to dispel them.

Gargoyle

Type	Alchemical Creation
Health	100-200
Soak	0/0/0
Damage	20–100 A
Special Attacks	None
Description	From the bodies of captured vampires, arises this ancient slave-race to the Tremere. They are powerful, if bestial creatures, rising above the height of man with great bat-like wings that spread from their shoulder blades.
Tactics	Gargoyles display a tremendous range in their physical abilities—identify the weaker ones and destroy them first while avoiding the attacks of their stronger brethren. (The weaker ones are smaller and more ratlike in appearance; the Greater Gargoyles look almost like lions!)

Demon Hound

Type	Possessed Animal
Health	60
Soak	0/0/0
Damage	50 A
Special Attacks	None
Description	A normal dog or wolf possessed by an infernal presence, these creatures appear monstrous.
Tactics	Although dangerous, these beasts possess little intelligence and no mystical powers.

Skeleton

Type	Undead
Health	60
Soak	0/50/50
Damage	45 L
Special Attacks	Bow
Description	The literal undead, a walking pile of human bones raised from the grave through necromantic rituals.
Tactics	Use bashing weapons to easily shatter these abominations' bones. (They are practically invulnerable to lethal and Aggravated damage.)

Elemental

Type	Summoned
Health	200
Soak	0/0/0
Damage	150 B
Special Attacks	None
Description	The living rock formed into humanoid shape and given animation through magic.
Tactics	Elementals are slow and tough. Expect them to absorb a lot of damage before they are broken into pieces. They will shatter though, so pound at them before they can bring their great strength to bear upon you!

Lawmen

Lawmen guard each city, protecting its civilians from criminals and creatures of the night alike. Should they see you attacking a townsperson (such as feeding upon them) or catch you in a vulgar display of supernatural powers, they will attack. Although it is possible to kill individual guards, they will summon aid and eventually overwhelm you with sheer numbers!

Knights of St. John (Prague Guards)

Type	Medieval Knights, human
Health	100
Soak	30/60/30
Damage	35–45 L
Special Attacks	None
Description	The guardians of Prague the Swordbrethren are vigorous crusaders, soldiers in heaven's army.

Vienna Guards

Type	Medieval Knights, human
Health	100
Soak	40/80/40
Damage	30-45 L
Special Attacks	Crossbow
Description	The Vienna guards are tougher than their Prague counterparts, but ill prepared to face creatures of the night. Many of them are in thrall to the Tremere.

Bobbies

Type	Police, human
Health	30
Soak	30/70/35
Damage	10 B
Special Attacks	None
Description	Nicknamed after Sir Robert Peel, the founder of London's metropolitan police force, the constabulary of England are poorly equipped to deal with the creatures of darkness.

NY's Finest

Type	Police/SWAT Team Human
Health	30
Soak	30/70/35
Damage	35 L +
Special Attacks	Firearms
Description	Contemporary American Police will respond with all the firepower and brutality expected of them.

Summoned Creatures

Using their occult powers, vampires may call upon the following creatures to help them fight (their statistics are identical to the normal versions shown earlier):

Viper	Dark Hunters	Wolves
Zombu	Rats	Szlachta
Hoppers	Skeletons	
Wraiths	Elementals	

Vampires

Vampires are divided by age—older vampires have more power. The following table provides age categories and their corresponding powers.

Title:	Health:	Blood:	Attributes:	Clan Disciplines:
Fledgling	50	50	20	1
Neonate	100	100	25-35	2
Ancilla	150	120	35–45	2-3
Elder	200	140	55-65	3-4
Methuselah	300	150	65-75+	4+

Individuals within each category may vary tremendously from these outlines.

Most vampires that the coterie fights will be in the mid-range, but it is impossible to tell from appearance what their age is. Individual vampires may be of a different gender (although this has no effect on their power) and may be equipped with a variety of weapons. In addition, vampires will wear armor, but again this varies from individual to individual. For example, the Cappadocians you meet early in the game have no armor, wearing only simple habits, while many vampires (such as the Setites in London and Giovanni in New York) wear armored vests beneath their clothes, giving them soak totals of 60/20/20.

Individual vampire clans use different names from those above. For example, the Tremere divide themselves between Apprentices, Lords, Regents, and Pontifexes.

Minor Bosses

These characters defend locations in the game, but are not directly related to your quests.

Othelios

Type	Nosferatu leader
Health	200
Soak	0/0/0
Damage	135 L
Special Attacks	Clan Nosferatu disciplines at level 4 (Common, Animalism, Obfuscate, and Potence)
Description	The emaciated form of this leper hides his tremendous strength. He carries a nasty axe with which he can easily strike you and your coterie down.
Tactics	Expect a high level of brutality here. The Nosferatu leader is powerful and dangerous, and you're not fighting him alone. He will not hesitate to feed upon your coterie, hurting them and draining precious blood with great speed. Make sure that Christof is carrying the Gangrel Eye so he can see this foe and concentrate your attacks upon him. Ensure that your coterie has plenty of blood—they'll need it. When you kill him, you are rewarded with his axe!

Dark Knight

Type	Teutonic Knight Boss
Description	The leader of the Teutonic Knights stands out in his blackened armor.
Health	70
Soak	60/80/30
Damage	100 L
Special Attacks	None
Weaknesses	Mortal
Tactics	Although more powerful than the rest of his knights, the Dark Knight is still merely mortal. Demonstrate your vampiric abilities to gain the upper hand in battle against him.

Virstania, Mistress of Gargoyles

Type	Tremere Leader
Description	A tall, pale woman in the finest robes, she fights with a barbed halberd.
Health	200
Soak	0/0/0
Damage	75 B
Powers	Virstania can use all the powers of the Tremere at level 3 (Common, Auspex, Dominate, and Blood Magic.) A powerful gargoyle will protect her.
Weaknesses	She will fight rather than use her disciplines.
Tactics	When Virstania wants to fight, oblige her. For all her arrogance, she is not equipped to resist your attacks and can be overwhelmed with ease.

Major Bosses

These enemies represent the fulfillment of a quest. They mark and guard the major story events in the game. As such, they are powerful foes and have many powers. Given that all of them have many attributes, they are resistant to many disciplines (such as Presence and Dominate). Although you may try controlling or clouding their minds, you are likely to fail and will most often be forced into a physical confrontation. Likewise, most of them are protected from being fed upon either through inherent power or mystical charms.

Be careful when fighting bosses—always make sure that your coterie is well armed and supplied with blood because these fights can be very challenging indeed!

Ahzra the Unliving

Type	Monstrous Vampire
Description	Ahzra is a Tzimisce vampire furthering her clan's conquest of Prague. She is hideously inhuman due to the use of the flesh-crafting powers of the discipline of Vicissitude and has the skin of a fallen werewolf foe wrapped about her shoulder.
Health	200
Soak	30/30/0
Damage	30 A
Powers	Ahzra can use Blood Healing, increase her strength with Blood Strength, and even summon szlachta to her side with the Beckoning.
Weaknesses	Ahzra is overconfident and will not use the full-range of her vampiric powers.
Tactics	Ahzra is a tough opponent and, unless you can weaken her fast by using any holy water or numina scrolls you have collected, it will be a very difficult fight. The best way to overcome her is to learn the pattern of her attacks, retreating as she prepares to bite and attacking her as she recovers. If you can keep her off-balance, it is possible to overwhelm her before she can kill you. Remember that healing salves take a short time to take effect, so use them in good time and pull away from her as you heal. You don't want to be using the potion just as she kills you!

Mercurio, Childe of Garinol

Type	Ambitious Vampire Necromancer
Description	Appearing as a humble monk, these humble trappings hide a rotten heart. Mercurio is unpreposing, except for the gleam of madness and ambition in his eyes.
Health	300
Soak	0/0/0
Damage	75 B
Powers	Cappadocian clan disciplines at level 3 (Common, Auspex, Mortis, Fortitude)
Weaknesses	Mercurio wears no armor, and this gives you a chance. Hit him hard with the best weapons you have and lure him into physical conflict.
Tactics	Make sure that Christof and Wilhem are attacking from opposite sides. If they are too close together, Mercurio can strike them both with Plague Wind or Black Death.

Maqqabah the Golem

Type	A kabalistic construct.
Description	A vast humanoid shape of earth and stone animated by magic. The golem feels no pain and is virtually indestructible.
Health	200
Soak	60/80/80
Damage	90 B
Powers	In addition to its sheer strength, Maqqabah can hurl an opponent into the air, smashing them down again into the ground.
Weaknesses	Slow movement
Tactics	Hit and run, and especially run if Maqqabah lifts his hands above his head (the preparation for his smash attack). Mental powers are very effective against the simple-witted beast, so use Awe to keep it confused and unable to focus its attacks upon you. Given that Maqqabah is a simple creature, it is possible that its attention will become focused on a single member of your coterie. If this becomes the case, a new tactic becomes available to you. Take control of the character the golem is focusing on, then run away making sure you are always close, but out of attack range of Maqqabah. The golem will continue to chase that one character, allowing the second member of your coterie to attack him from behind!

The Wraith of King Vaclav

Type	Insane spirit of the Dead
Description	A translucent, twisted figure that rises from the tomb to oppose you.
Health	200
Soak	Immune/60/60; Immune to Cold and Electricity
Damage	65 Cold
Powers	Vaclav carries with him the aura of death. He can drain your life-force (blood) and suck life (health) from you with a touch. He may also Call Lightning, Mesmerize, Heightened Senses, Heal, Strength, and use Theft of Vitae.
Weaknesses	Vaclav is bound to his tomb, so he cannot follow you. That means if things go badly, you can always just run!
Tactics	Back away, using any ranged attacks or disciplines to disable him. Vaclav is immune to mortal weapons, so this can be a very difficult fight. Vaclav is the first spirit you encounter on your journey. Spirits make dangerous opponents because they are immaterial and, hence, invulnerable to physical attacks. The only sure way to damage spirits is with Aggravated damage (such as that caused by Feral Claws) or by Elemental damage (fire, holy water, etc.) Whenever you fight spirits, make sure you have attacks that can harm them. Coterie members without such attacks should be pulled out of combat, or set to use mental powers that can distract the foe.

Ardan of Golden Lane

Type	Cowardly Vampire wizard
Description	Ardan wears the rich robes of a hermetic magus, elaborately embroidered with occult symbols. He is vain and cares only for his appearance, preferring to use words rather than force an issue to combat.
Health	200
Soak	30/30/30 +30 Soak vs. Fire, Electricity, and Cold
Damage	70 A
Powers	Ardan can summon fire and lightning, as well as influence the minds of his foes. He can Call Lightning and Mesmerize your coterie.
Weaknesses	Ardan is unprepared for physical combat, especially now that Erik has joined you, so you should be able to overwhelm him quickly.
Tactics	Rush him before he can gather his wits and either summon help or strike you with fire. Should he seize control over any members of your coterie, ignore them and concentrate your attacks on Ardan. His death will break the spell.

Erik the Gargoyle

Type	Transformed Ancient Gangrel
Description	As the Warlock's magic warps Erik's blood, he transforms into a powerful gargoyle. His red hair and beard become a leonine mane while his powerful body twists into a monstrous form and wings sprout from his shoulder blades.
Health	200
Soak	0/0/0
Damage	100 A
Powers	None
Weaknesses	The creature that once was Erik is in a bestial rage. It will not use disciplines against you.
Tactics	The being that once was Erik is in a bestial frenzy and you have no choice except to destroy him. He will concentrate his attacks on whomever hurts him the most, so use this to your advantage—make sure the first member of your coterie to attack him is the best armored and, therefore, able to stand toe-to-toe with Erik. The gargoyle will concentrate his attacks on that one person, leaving the others free to act.

Etrius of the Council of Seven

Type	Insanely Powerful Vampire Sorcerer
Description	Nothing prepared Etrius for eternity, and weariness shows in every line of his immortal face and body. He wears plain robes, preferring that his power show through without the need for ostentatious dress. His eyes reveal all one needs to know of damnation.
Health	200
Soak	30/30/30 +30 Soak vs. Fire, Electricity, and Cold
Damage	85 A
Powers	Etrius possesses all the powers of the lesser Tremere, but with centuries of experience, first as a mortal mage and now as the undead. His ability to manipulate the elements and the minds of his foes is unsurpassed (Feed 3, Blood Healing 3, Theft of Vitae 3, and Call Lightning 3).
Weaknesses	Etrius does not have time to deal with the intrusion. When the coterie's resistance proves stronger than expected, he will depart.
Tactics	Once Etrius starts spell casting, you have little chance. The best way to defeat him is to keep him constantly off-guard with melee attacks.

Father Leo Alotius

Type	Ghoul Fanatic
Description	Father Leo appears as a man in his late middle age. However, he is actually over two centuries old, having sustained himself on the blood of slain vampires. He is fanatically devoted to the Society and fails to see the redemptive chance in Christof.
Health	100
Soak	0/0/0
Damage	55 B
Powers	Father Leo is far stronger than any normal human and greatly skilled with his staff/walking cane.
Weaknesses	Leo is addicted to kindred blood that he keeps stored in vast vats in his study. If you destroy the vats, he will collapse helplessly.
Tactics	When it comes down to it, Father Leo is merely mortal. Christof is an elder vampire at this point, so use your powers or your physical prowess to overwhelm him.

Lucretia

Type	Ancient Vampire
Description	Lucretia styles herself after the ancient priestesses of the Nile that tended Set's reptilian servants. Her Egyptian garb is very revealing and she loves the shock value it has on opponents.
Health	250
Soak	60/60/60 +60 Soak vs. Fire, Electricity, and Cold
Damage	125 B
Powers	Setite Disciplines at level 3
Weaknesses	No powerful ranged attack.
Tactics	Overwhelm her with your attacks—if she charms any of your coterie, things can go very badly. Use firearms to keep her at a distance and prevent her from attacking you. Utilize the autofire feature to fire at her continuously.

Giant Cobra (Lucretia II)

Type	Transformed Vampire
Description	A giant snake, over twelve feet long.
Health	250
Soak	80/80/80 +100 Soak vs. Fire, Electricity, and Cold
Damage	140 A
Powers	Lucretia's cobra form is very fast and its poisonous bite can slay your coterie with ease. It has the powers of Feed, Blood Healing, Mesmerize, and the entire Serpentis discipline at level 3.
Weaknesses	None
Tactics	Lucretia's cobra form is deadly. You must damage it quickly to make sure it does not inflict serious damage on your coterie. Using fire weapons and explosives is very effective. Eventually, you will be able to attack her amanuensis. He will then drop her heart, which gives you power over her.

The Underprince

Type	Powerful vampire with a swarm of rabid rats.
Description	A bloated, twisted shape in a stained and soiled suit long out of fashion, the Underprince is the undisputed ruler of the downtown portion of the New York sewer system.
Health	100
Soak	40/40/40
Damage	60 A
Powers	Nosferatu level 3-4 (Common, Potence, Animalism, and Obfuscate.)
Weaknesses	Too arrogant to use obfuscate.
Tactics	Ignore the rats—the Underprince can always call on more. Concentrate your attacks on the Underprince himself. Use explosives or fire to clear a path through to him.

Count Orsi (modern)

Type	Vampire Degenerate
Description	The years have been good to Orsi—he is every inch a prosperous man in his tailored three-piece suit and hair tied back in a neat ponytail. The slave-master has become a respected businessman.
Health	100
Soak	30/30/30
Damage	85 L
Powers	Ventrue clan disciplines at level 4 (Common, Dominate, Fortitude, and Presence.)
Weaknesses	Orsi is weak. He is essentially a fop and ill-suited to fighting the entire coterie. Rush him and overwhelm him so that he cannot use any of his mental disciplines to turn your characters on each other.
Tactics	Payback!

Vukodlak, Voivode of Voivodes, Master of the Cathedral of Flesh

Type	Ancient Vampire
Description	Taller than any man, Vukodlak's form has been sculpted into that of a hellish beast. His eyes burn with power and his voice is death. The robes he wears thankfully conceal the true extent of this monstrosity.
Health	550
Soak	100/100/100 +100 Soak vs. Fire, Electricity, and Cold
Damage	170 A
Powers	In addition to his extraordinary physical power, the Voivode can call on the powers of koldunic sorcery to steal blood from his foes, as well as command the elements to strike them dead. (Common, Animalism, Blood Magic, and Call Lightning at 4 or 5!)
Weaknesses	None
Tactics	Hit Vukodlak with everything you have—any of his attacks are sufficient to torpor a coterie member, so attack him relentlessly. Use any high explosives or powerful flame weapons you have and burn blood like it's going out of fashion. Because of the Voivode's immense soak totals, you must activate disciplines such as Potence to stand a real chance of harming him—un-enhanced attacks are easily deflected by his tough skin and mystical protections.

Vukodlak in Zulo Form

Type	Ancient Vampire in battle-form, a horror out of the past.
Description	With his mastery of Koldunic sorcery complete, Vukodlak can call on all the power of the Tzimisce to transform himself into their ancient battle-form. Flaunting a vast, long-limbed body with wings, a barbed tail, and a head close to the terrible lizards of a bygone age, the Zulo form is an expression of his ultimate mastery over the flesh and rejection of the human form!
Health	550
Soak	100/100/100 +100 Soak vs. Fire, Electricity, and Cold
Damage	140 B
Powers	The Zulo form is the ancient battle-form of the Voivode. A nightmare killing machine, Vukodlak maintains his mind and can use his terrible sorcery in this form. (Common, Animalism, Blood Magic, and Call Lightning at 4 or 5!)
Weaknesses	None
Tactics	This is the last stand for Christof's soul—and the fate of humanity. Use everything you have immediately. Should Vukodlak win, the eternal night will fall.

Arms & Equipment

There are many items you can find in the game that will help your quest and increase your chance of survival. Here are a few gameplay notes before we get into the specifics of each weapon, piece of armor, and unique item.

How Attacks are Calculated

A character's chance to hit an opponent is calculated by comparing their Dexterity and the weapon's Accuracy trait against the foe's Dexterity. The opposing traits are randomized and a result is reached: If the attacker was particularly successful they may score a critical hit, which inflicts greater damage and may have secondary effects—for example, staking with a wooden stake or decapitating a foe with an edged weapon.

What the Damage Traits Mean

There are three core types of damage in the game: Bashing (**B**), Lethal (**L**), and Aggravated(**A**). Bashing damage is inflicted with blunt weapons or hand-to-hand combat, and is the least damaging of the three classes—commonly bruising and more rarely breaking bones. Lethal damage is inflicted with slashing or cutting weapons, and causes open bleeding wounds. Aggravated damage is inflicted only by supernatural or elemental means, and is the hardest to resist. Mortals can add to their Stamina to soak rolls against Bashing. Cainites and other supernaturals can soak both Bashing and Lethal with their Stamina. However, no one has innate resistance to Aggravated damage. In addition to these core damage types, there are specific elemental effects, all of which are Aggravated. These are Fire, Cold, Electricity, Faith, and Sunlight. Such elemental damage affects different characters individually. For example, humans are not damaged by Sunlight or Holy attacks.

What the Soak Traits Mean

There is a soak trait for each damage type. The higher this trait is, the more damage your character will 'soak' from an incoming attack. Soak totals are divided into three core areas (Bashing, Lethal, and Aggravated), as well as Elemental Attacks (Faith, Fire, Cold, Electricity, and Sunlight). This division is to allow for the differences between mortals and immortals, as well as between different classes of supernatural creatures. For example, vampires are vulnerable to sunlight, but humans are not.

How Damage is Calculated

Damage is calculated by comparing the attacker's Damage trait to the defender's Soak trait. Basically, damage for melee weapons is Base Damage + Strength, and for ranged attacks it is Base Damage unmodified. So if your character has 10 Strength and is wielding a broadsword (30 L), they will do 40 Lethal damage. This damage is randomized and compared to the enemy's soak totals (also randomized) to derive the damage you actually inflict.

Weapons

There are numerous weapons at your disposal in *Vampire: The Masquerade - Redemption*. The following is a breakdown of each instrument of battle and how they are classified.

Classes

Individual weapons may be altered to change their abilities. The special classes of weapons you may find include:

Class:	Effect:
Rusty	-5 Damage
Fine	+5 Damage
Exquisite	+10 Damage, +5 Accuracy
Dread	Extra damage and Accuracy; may cause fear in your enemies.
Berserk	Extra damage and Accuracy, but causes Frenzy in its wielder.
Flaming	Inflicts Aggravated Fire Damage.
Poisoned	+35 Poison Damage (this replaces the weapon's usual damage).
Blessed	Inflicts Holy damage (Aggravated), requires Faith to wield.

I-H Slashing/Stabbing Weapons

Weapon:	Damage:	Accuracy:	Speed:	Requirements:	Description:
Dagger	10 L	15	133	None	The standard medieval knife.
Poignard	20 L	10	133	None	With its thinner blade, this lighter version of the dagger is favored by assassins.
Moro Dagger	20 L	0	133	None	The serrated blade inflicts greater damage and is ideal for getting poison into an enemy's system.
Dirk	15 L	0	133	None	The northern variant of the dagger, its traits are identical.

I-H Slashing/Stabbing Weapons (continued)

Weapon:	Damage:	Accuracy:	Speed:	Requirements:	Description:
Saber/Rapier	25 L	25	99	None	The classic weapon of fencers and cavalry. An elegant blade with increased Accuracy.
Broadsword	30 L	0	90	None	The classic weapon of the medieval knight, skill in the sword separates the nobility from the peasant.
Scythe	25 L	0	66	None	A wicked adaptation of the farming tool, the scythe is used by those vampires that desire fashion over effectiveness.
Flamberge	40 L	10	99	STR>25	Heavier and more accurate than the broadsword, this weapon is favored by mercenaries and scoundrels.
Scimitar	30 L	0	99	None	The Middle Eastern sword is broader and heavier than its European counterpart. A good all-around weapon.
Hand Axe	25 L	0	99	None	A peasant weapon favored by woodsmen.
Falchion	35 L	+15	99	None	Another sword variant, this one has an extended hilt for extra power and control. Used most often by Germanic knightly orders, it never gains the widespread popularity of the broadsword due to the increased training time required to learn how to wield it.

2-H Slashing/Stabbing Weapons

Weapon:	Damage:	Accuracy:	Speed:	Requirements:	Description:
Bastard Sword	40 L	0	83	STR>35	Also known as the hand-and-a-half sword because of its extended hilt, it is the easiest of the two-handed swords to wield.
Greatsword	60 L	0	76	STR>45	A huge weapon that few mortals could ever wield, it inflicts tremendous damage on your foes.
Bastion	60 L	0	71	STR>35	A large poleaxe ending in a wicked blade.
Lance	65 L	0	71	STR>40	Normally used on horseback, only the strongest mortal could hope to wield this in combat—a restriction that applies far less to the Kindred.
Spear	30 L	0	76	STR>25	The basic infantry weapon down the ages.
Pitchfork	20 L	0	99	STR>25	When the peasants storm the castle, no other weapon will do!
Claymore	45 L	0	83	STR>35	This weapon, favored by the Scottish clans, inflicts tremendous damage when it connects.
Halberd	45 L	0	76	STR>25	Perhaps the most common poleaxe, it is favored by Swiss mercenaries and any other trained infantry squad.
Battleaxe	65 L	0	71	STR>45	When you want to make sure your enemy does not get up, this is the weapon of choice.
Poleaxe	55 L	0	76	STR>25	Used by guards in castles across Europe, this weapon is neither fast nor elegant, but keeps an enemy away from you.

I-H Blunt Weapons

Weapon:	Damage:	Accuracy:	Speed:	Requirements:	Description:
Club	20 B	10	90	None	A basic stick, this is most often a makeshift weapon rather than a prized possession.
Mace	30 B	0	90	None	A heavy ball of metal at the end of a short shaft. Ideal for bashing in the heads of annoying knights.
Flanged Mace	30 B	10	90	None	Lighter and more effective than the standard mace, its flanged edges allow it to break armor with more ease.

2-H Blunt Weapons

Weapon:	Damage:	Accuracy:	Speed:	Requirements:	Description:
Quarterstaff	35 B	0	90	STR>25	A stout oaken staff as long as a man is tall.
Spiked Mace	50 B	0	76	STR>40	A heavy spiked iron ball at the end of a four-foot shaft. Nasty!
Warhammer	55 B	0	76	STR>45	Designed to knock armored foes to the ground, whereupon you can use the hammer to pry open their armor.

Modern Weapons

Melee Weapons

Weapon:	Damage:	Accuracy:	Speed:	Requirements:	Description:
Broken Bottle	20 B	0	99	None	Favorite of barroom brawlers, this is generally an ineffective weapon.
Baseball Bat	25 B	0	85	None	In the tradition of Al Capone, a baseball bat is the mobster weapon of choice.
Brass Knuckles	5 B	0	99	None	Used by brawlers to increase their damage, brass knuckles do not increase your chance of survival greatly.
Chainsaw	75 L	0	49	STR>25	The classic horror film weapon is hard to control, but inflicts tremendous damage on opponents.
Lead Pipe	10 B	0	99	None	Another makeshift weapon of limited value.
Machete	20 L	0	99	None	This jungle blade sees its use amongst the Setites.
Sap Gloves	10 B	0	99	None	Gloves lined with lead or sand to increase punching damage.

Firearms

Modern firearms can inflict damage at great speed. Vampires are more resistant to their effects than mortals, but can still be put down by sustained fire.

Weapon:	Damage:	Accuracy:	Speed:	Ammo:	Requirements:	Description:
Pistol	55 B	20	75	11	None	The standard sidearm of security forces worldwide.
Dragonsbreath Pistol(Fire)	55 A	20	75	11	Unique rounds	A modified pistol that fires incendiary rounds.
Rifle	60 B	30	49	22	None	Used by snipers and hunters, this weapon is accurate, but has a low rate of fire.
Revolver	65 B	25	75	6	None	The classic police special.
Taser	10	0	99	N/A	None	For self defense only.

Firearms (continued)

Weapon:	Damage:	Accuracy:	Speed:	Ammo:	Requirements:	Description:
Electrical Incinerator	30 FIRE	0	33	20	None	A one-handed flame-thrower; very dangerous to Kindred.
Submachine Gun	55 B	5	75	32	None	Used by security forces world wide, the most famous of these is the Uzi used by Israeli security.
Assault Rifle	45 B	15	66	40	STR>25	A military weapon capable of firing a large amount of ammunition in a very short time.
Rocket Launcher	250 FIRE	15	75	3	STR>25	A fully military weapon capable of delivering its payloads across extreme ranges. It is very, very dangerous in close quarters.
Grenade Launcher	200 FIRE	0	75	20	STR>25	Fires standard offensive grenades. Be careful not to get caught in the splash radius or by a ricochet.
Shotgun	75 B	15	75	20	None	The takedown weapon, used to clear out rooms by SWAT teams.
Chaingun	30 B	0	40	10	STR>40	The ultimate military weapon, for when everyone in the room has to die now!
Flamethrower	40 FIRE	0	33	20	STR>30	A military weapon designed to produce a steady stream of fire under all conditions.
Stakegun	40 B	15	75	20	None	A heavily modified air gun with a rotating ammo drum, this strange weapon can fire wooden stakes at high velocity into the target.

Altered Firearms

Modified	Increased Damage: +10
Sighted	Increased Accuracy: +5

Ranged Weapons

Bows & Crossbows

Although primarily medieval weapons, bows still find their enthusiasts in the modern nights.

Weapon:	Damage:	Accuracy:	Speed:	Ammo:	Requirements:	Description:
Compound Bow	35 L	20	75	20	DEX+STR>25	A modern bow made from layered woods and plastics to create increased tensile strength and more damaging and accurate fire.
Crossbow	35 L	0	120	20	None	The terror of the medieval battlefield, this weapon was declared Anathema by the Pope in the Eleventh Century.
Long Bow	30 L	0	75	20	DEX+STR>25	The weapon of the Welsh on the battlefield, it won Agincourt for the English.
Modern X-Bow	35 L	10	120	20	None	Another modern weapon, this is the classic enhanced by modern technology.
Short Bow	30 L	0	75	20	DEX>25	The bow of the horseman fires smaller arrows with greater speed.

Specially Altered Bows

Each of these modified bows requires specific ammo and cannot be fired with a normal bow.

Modification:	Ammo:
Silver	Specially-made silver arrows (Aggravated damage to Werewolves)
Incendiary	Flaming arrows (Aggravated fire damage)
Magnesium	Magnesium tipped bolts and arrows (Aggravated fire damage)

Grenades and Explosives

These thrown weapons rely on muscle power to deliver their payload to a target. Most of them are explosive and dangerous in close quarters. They all share the same traits, with some minor variation. Each can be prepped and used once.

Greek Fire

Holy Water (Holy Damage, not Fire)

Concussion Grenade

White Phosphorous Grenade

Chemical Grenade

Satchel Charge

Napalm Bomb

Fragmentation Grenade

Damage	Aggravated damage (varies by type from 30 for Greek Fire up to 200 for Satchel Charges)
Accuracy	0
Speed	60
Description	Creates an explosion around the target character, inflicting damage on all within a small radius. A character badly hurt by fire may catch on fire and continue to burn (taking damage) for some seconds after the initial impact.

Throwing Knives

Knives and Shuriken share the same traits. Generally, when you find either of these weapons you do not find a single one, but rather several individual weapons. As such, both have an Ammo trait, indicating the number of blades you have. You can use the item until its 'ammo' is exhausted.

Damage	20 L
Accuracy	15
Speed	60

Special Weapons

Weapon:	Damage:	Accuracy:	Speed:	Requirements:	Description:
Stake	5-20 B	15	95	None	The vampire hunter's friend, it may stake a Cainite opponent on a critical hit.

Armor

There are many types of armor to be found in the game. They all provide protection against hard fate.

Modified Armor

Blessed/Holy	Soaks Aggravated damage; Faith minimum to equip.
Unholy	Soak Faith damage in addition to normal soaks.
Grounded	+10 Soak vs. Electricity
Insulated	+10 Soak vs. Fire, Cold, or Sunlight (varies by item!)

Enchanted Gauntlets

These provide additional bonuses. Each gauntlet you find is actually a pair, occupying both of your character's arm slots in their inventory.

Accuracy Gauntlets	Increases your chance of making a successful attack.
Gauntlets of Dexterity	Increases your Dexterity attribute.
Dodging Gauntlets	Increases your chance to evade blows in combat.
Fortitude Gauntlets	Adds to your soak totals.
Power Gauntlets	Extra damage to your attacks.
Gauntlets of Strength	Increases your Strength attribute.
Gauntlets of Stamina	Increases your Stamina attribute.

Medieval Armor

Helms

Armor:	Soak:
Skullcap	Bashing +10 / Lethal +10 / Aggravated +10
Light Helm	Bashing +15 / Lethal +15 / Aggravated +15
Full Helm	Bashing +30 / Lethal +30 / Aggravated +20

Sets/Body

Armor:	Soak:	Requirements:
Rags	Bashing +5 / Lethal +5 / Aggravated +0	N/A
Padded Clothing	Bashing +10 / Lethal +10 / Aggravated +10	N/A
Leather Armor	Bashing +10 / Lethal +15 / Aggravated +10 / Fire +10 / Electricity +10	N/A
Studded Leather	Bashing +15 / Lethal +30 / Aggravated +15 / Fire +10 / Electricity +3	N/A
Chainmail	Bashing +15 / Lethal +45 / Aggravated +20	STR>25
Scale Mail	Bashing +15 / Lethal +45 / Aggravated +20	STR>25
Chest Plate	Bashing +30 / Lethal +30 / Aggravated +15	N/A
Half Plate	Bashing +30 / Lethal +60 / Aggravated +25	STR>35
Plate Mail	Bashing +30 / Lethal +80 / Aggravated +30	STR>45
Leather Gloves	Bashing +5 / Lethal +5 / Aggravated +0	N/A

Shields

Armor:	Soak:	Requirements:
Buckler	Bashing +10 / Lethal +10 / Aggravated +10	N/A
Shield	Bashing +15 / Lethal +15 / Aggravated +15	N/A
Footman's Shield	Bashing +30 / Lethal +30 / Aggravated +20	N/A
Cavalry Shield	Bashing +30 / Lethal +30 / Aggravated +20	N/A
Norman Shield	Bashing +30 / Lethal +30 / Aggravated +20	STR>25
Great Shield	Bashing +30 / Lethal +30 / Aggravated +20	STR>35

Special

Armor:	Soak:	Special:
Neckguard	None	Protects wearer from the fangs of vampires.

Modern Armor

Helms

Armor:	Soak:
Army Helm	Bashing +10 / Lethal +10 / Aggravated +10
SWAT Helmet	Bashing +10 / Lethal +10 / Aggravated +10
Motorcycle Helmet	Bashing +10 / Lethal +10 / Aggravated +10
Light Enhancing Goggles	Although the goggles offer no protection, they do improve vision, giving characters a chance to spot hidden or obfuscated enemies.

Sets/Body

Armor:	Soak:
Leather jacket	Bashing +15 / Lethal +10 / Aggravated +10
Armor T-shirt	Bashing +30 / Lethal +10 / Aggravated +10
Tailored Armor	Bashing +80 / Lethal +45 / Aggravated +25
Fire Resistant Armor*	Bashing +10 / Lethal +10 / Aggravated +10
Flak Jacket	Bashing +45 / Lethal +10 / Aggravated +10
Reinforced Clothing	Bashing +10 / Lethal +10 / Aggravated +10
Leather Vest	Bashing +10 / Lethal +10 / Aggravated +10
Light Ballistic Vest	Bashing +30 / Lethal +15 / Aggravated +15
Medium Ballistic Vest	Bashing +45 / Lethal +30 / Aggravated +20
Tactical Jacket	Bashing +60 / Lethal +45 / Aggravated +25

* SPECIAL: Soak Fire +40

Gloves

Armor:	Soak:	Special:
Grounded Gloves	Bashing +0 / Lethal +0 / Aggravated +0	Soak Electricity +5

Shields

Armor:	Soak:
Riot Shield	Bashing +60 / Lethal +30 / Aggravated +20

Items

Light Sources

Item:	Function:
Torch	Illuminates the area around your character; equip in shield slot.
Flashlight	Illuminates the area around your character; equip in shield slot.

Treasure and Loot

Costume Jewelry

These items grant an appearance increase to the wearer, as well as being worth a significant amount of money. Each may be equipped in the appropriated inventory slots. Gold is worth more than silver, and diamond is more valuable than gold.

Jewelry:	Varieties:
Rings	Silver, Gold, and Diamond
Necklaces	Silver, Gold, and Diamond
Bracelets	Silver, Gold, and Diamond

Treasure

There is much treasure in the game that adds cash directly to your reserves or represents negotiable sources of wealth.

Cash can be found in the form of Silver Coins, Gold Coins, Pouches of Coins, and modern currency (cash). Items that can be sold for money include Rubies, Sapphires, Emeralds, Diamonds, Gold Bullion, and Bonds.

Mystical Items

These items are the product of both mortal alchemy and kindred blood magic.

Potions

Potions come in a variety of vials, bottles, and flasks. When consumed, they immediately have a positive effect on your character. To drink a potion, right-click on it in your inventory or quick slots.

Potion Type:	Effect:
Potions of Health: Ointment/Elixir/Salve	These potions, usable by mortals only, give you the limited ability to regenerate damage. For a short time, your character's health bar will rise as the potion courses through their system. Each successive healing potion lasts for slightly longer than its predecessor.
Potion of Mana	This potion, usable by mortals only, adds +30 Mana.
Potions of Cure Poison/Anti-toxin	This potion will purge your blood of any poison.
Potion of Cure Disease/Vaccine	This potion will cure you of any disease.

Blood Sources

These items are usable only by Kindred and add directly to your character's temporary Blood Pool when used. To use one, simple right-click on it in your inventory.

Source:	Effect:
Rat	+10
Bottle of Vitae	+25
Plasma Bag	+40
Blood Pouch	+55
Kindred Vitae	+55
Blood Pearl	+55
Fae Vitae	+70
Elder Vitae	+70
Blood Stone	+70
Antediluvian Blood	+100
Werewolf Blood	+100

Blood pouches are a special source of vitae—they contain several draughts of blood and can be used more than once before they are exhausted. You may also find other blood types with stranger effects, such as Giant's Blood (+5 Potence for a short time). Also note that the more powerful types of Vitae may provide additional powers to your characters.

There may be more types of blood in the game, such as Anathema blood and the fabled Concoction. Good luck finding them, and have fun experimenting with their effects!

Scrolls

Scrolls contain the power of a single Discipline or Numina. These items can each be used once, without costing your character any blood or mana.

To use a scroll, equip it and then right-click on it from your inventory. The scroll icon now becomes your cursor. Move it over a valid target in the game window and right-click. Once its power has been expended, the scroll vanishes. You can return a readied scroll to your inventory by left-clicking on an empty space within your backpack.

Tomes

These mystical books contain the distilled knowledge from centuries of study amongst the Children of Caine. Each grants the reader the ability to use a new Discipline group. To study a tome, right-click on it in your inventory.

There is a tome for each Discipline Group.

Mystical Jewelry

Mystical jewelry imparts bonuses to its wearers. To use one of these mystical items, equip it in the correct inventory slot. Such items can be divided into the three following categories:

Category:	Effect:
Discipline	Decreases the blood cost for casting disciplines.
Serenity	Decreases the Frenzy trait in the wearer.
Blood	Increases the bloodpool of the wearer.

You can also find rings and amulets (necklaces) that grant bonus to your character's attributes. There are rings and amulets of Intelligence, Perception, Wits, Charisma, and Manipulation.

Mortal Holy Artifacts

Holy Items

Holy items are usable only by human characters. They impart the power of faith, increasing the character's Faith trait.

Item:	Requirements:
Holy Cross	May be worn about the neck.
Holy Star of David	May be worn about the neck.
Holy Statuette	Must be equipped in the character's shield hand.

Holy Artifacts

These items are unique. Each is a treasured work of art, jealously guarded by its owner. They impart great power to the wielder and are part of the vast scope of Kindred history.

Artifact:	Type:	Damage:	Special:	Description:
The Ainkurn Sword	Sword Two-Handed	45A	+10 DEX	Legend has it that this baneful weapon was bathed in the blood of an antediluvian as it was forged. Some say it retains the spirit and thirsts of its smith. Random Chance to steal blood from an enemy and transfer it into wielder's blood pool.
Ivory Bow	Bow	75 L	High damage	A bow made of purest ivory, it is enchanted to do great damage.
Black Gloves	Glove Slot	N/A	(See next page*)	Made by a fashion conscious Toreador, these gloves grant the wearer the ability to tremendous damage with their bare hands!
Monocle of Clarity	Head Slot	N/A	True Seeing (5)	Created by the Tremere to detect Nosferatu spies, the Monocle grants enhanced perceptions to its user.
Gangrel Eye	Utility/Shield	N/A	Eyes of the Beast (5)	An eye torn from an ancient Gangrel warlord and enchanted with mystical properties.

Holy Artifacts (continued)

Artifact:	Type:	Damage:	Special:	Description:
Hand of Conrad	Weapon	30 A	Potence (3)	The hand and arm of a great warrior preserved through necromancy, it grants great strength to its wielder.
The Femur of Elder Tzimisce	Weapon	20 A	Extra damage vs. vampires	The leg-bone of an elder Tzimisce wrapped in enchantments and made into a weapon.
Heart Plate	Armor (Body)	N/A	100% protection against staking	Made from the flesh of an extinct beast, this grotesque chest plate protects its wearer from being staked.
Sire's Finger	Shield/Utility	N/A	Reduces frenzy by 50%	A strange and unholy item, this finger of an ancient vampire compels those who hold it to think dispassionately. Some legends say it is Brujah's finger, others that it is a product of magic pure and simple.
Argent Baton	Weapon	20 B	Extra damage vs. werewolves	Designed to slay moonbeasts by playing on their vulnerability to silver and their link to the lunar cycles, this weapon is a prized possession.
Cloak of Shadows	Armor body	N/A	Obfuscate (3)	A cloak of gossamer threads that seems to whisper with the voices of the departed, it cloaks the wearer in deep shadows.
Berserker Fang	Weapon	30 A	A fast, Aggravated attack	The tooth of a fallen werewolf enchanted into a weapon.

* **Black Gloves Special:** Feral Claws permanently (character inflicts 15 A damage). However, once you have donned the gloves, you are unable to use other shape-changing disciplines, such as Mist Form, unless you first remove the gloves.

Kine Artifacts

These items are for the use of humans in multiplayer games.

Garou's Claw

The Matyr's Fire

The Dolorous Nail

Oil of St.George

Orb of Ulain

Ring of Chrysotom

Dagger of Thorns

Griffin Ring

Disciplines

Disciplines are the powers of the blood used by the children of Caine in their eternal battles. Humans can counter these advantages with the powers of Faith and Numina, psychic abilities.

A character's clan defines access to these powers—each clan of vampires specializes in certain abilities (the enemies you meet in the game will be primarily limited to their clan disciplines, although exceptions exist). In addition, all vampires have access to the Common group, which consists of the basic powers granted by the blood of Caine.

Clan:	Powers:
Assamite*	Celerity, Obfuscate, Quietus*
Brujah	Celerity, Potence, Presence
Caitiff	Any
Cappadocian	Auspex, Fortitude, Mortis
Gangrel	Animalism, Fortitude, Protean
Giovanni	Dominate, Mortis, Potence
Lasombra	Dominate, Obtenebration, Potence
Malkavian	Dementation, Obfuscate
Nosferatu	Animalism, Obfuscate, Potence
Ravnos*	Animalism, Chimestry*, Fortitude
Setite	Presence, Serpentis
Toreador	Auspex, Celerity, Presence
Tremere	Auspex, Dominate, Blood Magic
Tzimisce	Animalism, Auspex, Fortitude, Vicissitude*
Ventrue	Dominate, Fortitude, Presence

* These clans and their respective specialties are not in the Redemption chronicle. You may, however, encounter members of these clans in multiplayer games or future expansions.

The Giovanni refer to the discipline of mortis as Necromancy. They believe they have refined the Cappadocian clan discipline in the centuries since the destruction and diablerie of Cappadocius by Augusto Giovanni.

The Tremere are another special case. They believe that the discipline they call Thaumaturgy encompasses all the possible magics of the blood. As such, they not only use Blood Magic, but also Lure of Flames, Blood Rituals, and more rarely Hands of Destruction. Older kindred know that the Tremere were not the first to discover the magic inherent in the blood and remember the magic of the Assamites, Setites, and Tzimisce as well. A good example of such 'other magic' is the Koldunic sorcery used by Vukodlak in his quest for deification.

Common Disciplines

Feed

Blood Cost	0
Requirements	None
Effect	Allows you to draw blood from the target.
Tips	The primary use of feeding is, obviously, to replenish your coterie's blood supply. You can use this discipline on innocent humans, enemies, or in desperate straits, even members of your own coterie. Simply highlight the person you want to feed off of, then activate the discipline. Your character will make an attempt to grab them—this attempt may fail, but if it succeeds, the target is helpless until you release them or they expire from loss of blood. Because feeding will incapacitate any enemy, it is useful in combat. You are far more likely to miss an opponent who is actively guarding against you, so it makes sense to use Feed in combination with other powers. Perhaps the most effective combination is using Awe or Mesmerize to render a target quiescent—if an enemy is under the effect of such mental control, they will not be able to resist you.

Blood Healing

Blood Cost	5
Requirements	None
Effect	Heals 5 health per level.
Tips	The healing effect of Blood Healing is not instantaneous; instead, it is a steady regeneration that takes place over time. As such, it is important to activate this discipline early enough so that it takes full effect. The maximum amount of health it can restore is 25, so use it whenever a character drops toward half their maximum health. If you wait until your health is critically low, your character may be killed before the healing power has run its course.

Blood Strength

Blood Cost	5
Requirements	None
Effect	Adds 5 times level to your Strength Attribute with extended duration at higher levels.
Tips	The additional points of Strength gained through this discipline are identical in function to the character's natural attribute. Thus, they not only increase the damage your character inflicts in combat, but also allow you to wield heavier weapons and don bulkier armor.

Blood Dexterity

Blood Cost	5
Requirements	Blood Strength
Effect	Adds 5 times level to your Dexterity Attribute with extended duration at higher levels.
Tips	The additional points of Dexterity gained through this discipline are identical in function to the character's natural attribute. This increases your base chance to strike an opponent in combat, increasing your defenses against their attacks, as well as improving your chance of inflicting a critical attack. This can be particularly useful against bosses or if you are wielding a special weapon such as a stake.

Blood Stamina

Blood Cost	5
Requirements	Blood Dexterity
Effect	Adds 5 times level to your Stamina Attribute with extended duration at higher levels.
Tips	The additional points of Stamina gained through this discipline are identical in function to the character's natural attribute. As such, using this discipline increases your ability to soak all damage except for Aggravated damage—you must use Fortitude to further boost your defenses to do that!

Awaken

Blood Cost	15
Requirements	None
Effect	Revives an allied vampire from Torpor. You can target either their dead body or activate the power on their character portrait to use.
Tips	This discipline uses the power of the blood to call an ally back from Torpor. Its use is obvious and you should make sure that Christof develops this power as soon as possible so that you can revive fallen coterie members.

Walk the Abyss

Blood Cost	10
Requirements	Intelligence>25, Wits>25. Must have a Haven on the hub.
Effect	Opens a mystical portal between your current location and your Haven.
Tips	This strange power calls upon the bond between a vampire and his sleeping place to open a two-way portal between them. When activated, a glowing portal opens at your current location. When you step through it, you are immediately carried to your Haven. The other end of the portal will carry you back to your original location when you're finished in your Haven. This power will allow you to leave a dungeon at any point, rest and spend experience in your Haven (and even leave your haven to go shopping or to feed), and then return to the point where you left. Enemies cannot follow through the portal, so it is an easy escape route, giving you time to regain your strength.

Failing Power

There are certain times when Walk the Abyss will always fail—if you do not have a Haven, or if the area you are in is mystically shielded. A good example of this circumstance in the Redemption chronicle is the Teutonic Knight Base, which the Tremere have sealed shut; and the Society of Leopold in London where you do not have a Haven.

Physical Disciplines

CELERITY

Blood Cost	5
Requirements	None
Effect	Grants your character superhuman speed.
Tips	Use this not only for covering ground faster, but also to increase your attack speed. A good tactic when using this power is to attack your opponents and then dodge away—they will not have the speed to track your movements. This is especially useful against opponents with ranged attacks—it may even be possible to dodge speeding bullets!

FORTITUDE

Blood Cost	10
Requirements	None
Effect	Grants your character superhuman resistance to injury, including Aggravated damage.
Tips	Fortitude is similar to armor—it grants increased soak totals against all forms of damage. It is best to activate this when you know a tough fight (for example, against a boss) is coming up and you want to be able to resist attacks. It adds to your pre-existing soak totals, so you can make your character practically invulnerable through use of this discipline.

POTENCE

Blood Cost	5
Requirements	None
Effect	Grants your character superhuman strength.
Tips	The main use of Potence is in combat; not only does it increase your character's damage range, it also grants automatic damage successes that allow you to crush opponents. It is particularly effective when used in combat with another damage-enhancing discipline, such as Blood Strength or Feral Claws. The latter being particularly nasty, as you will inflict enhanced Aggravated damage.

Combining Powers

Celerity, Potence, and Fortitude can be grouped together—they enhance your character's physical prowess, enabling them to perform superhuman feats.

ANIMALISM

Feral Whispers

Blood Cost	5
Requirements	Manipulation > 25
Effect	This creates a bond between the caster and animals, making them fight at your side for a short time.
Tips	This power is seldom used, as most of the enemies you encounter are not vulnerable to its effects. It can be useful in turning the tide of battle if your foe has many pets, but is otherwise extremely limited. You can press the TAB key at any time to return to your body and relinquish control over your victim.

Beckoning

Blood Cost	10
Requirements	Charisma > 25
Effect	Summons an 'animal' ally to fight at your side with extended duration at higher levels.
Tips	The Beckoning creates a temporary servant based on clan affiliation; those clans removed from nature summon such things as skeletons and szlachta. The summoned creature is not a particularly effective fighter at higher levels, but can serve as a distraction to enemies. See the *Bestiary* chapter for details on summoned pets.

Quell the Beast

Blood Cost	10
Requirements	Manipulation > 50
Effect	This power reduces the Frenzy trait in a friend.
Tips	The use of this discipline is reactive—if an ally is frenzying, or in danger of frenzying, use this power to calm them down. It quickly reduces their Frenzy trait so that the madness passes quickly.

Subsume the Spirit

Blood Cost	15
Requirements	Manipulation > 60
Effect	Allows you to seize control of an animal for a short period of time.
Tips	Given the rarity of animals that associate with vampires, this power is seldom useful; however, it can be devastating. When used, you gain complete control over the target, moving it as if it were your character. For the duration of the power, you can make the victim do *anything*, including attack its own allies. You can press the TAB key at any time to return to your body and relinquish control over your victim.

Drawing Out the Beast

Blood Cost	20
Requirements	Manipulation > 70
Effect	Provokes Frenzy in an opponent.
Tips	This power is most useful when cast against an opponent who is less physically inclined and more likely to use powers or ranged weapons. Once they are in thrall to the Beast, they will attack in melee only, ignoring the other options. If it is used on an enemy amidst a group of foes, it turns them on each other, totally disrupting their effectiveness.

AUSPEX

Heightened Senses

Blood Cost	5
Requirements	Perception > 25
Effect	Increases the vampire's perceptions to superhuman levels.
Tips	The prime use of this power is to detect Invisible or Obfuscated enemies. If you have Heightened Senses activated, it automatically subtracts from the level of Obfuscate used by your foes, revealing them to your eyes. For example, if you are fighting a Nosferatu with Obfuscate 2 and you have Heightened Senses 2, you will always see them once this power is active (2 – 2 = 0.) For more details see *Obfuscate*.

Aura Perception

Blood Cost	5
Requirements	Perception > 35
Effect	This allows you to read the aura of one person.
Tips	This power is most useful in multiplayer games where aura reading may be useful to solving the plot or detecting traitors. The information it reveals is never critical in the Redemption chronicle.

Spirit's Touch

Blood Cost	10
Requirements	Perception > 30
Effect	This power exposes the hidden properties of items, revealing their secrets.
Tips	Use this power to reveal the hidden powers of 'unidentified' objects that you find. To use it, activate the power and then click on an unidentified object in your inventory with the targeting cursor that appears. Once you do this, the object's hidden powers will be revealed.

Psychic Projection

Blood Cost	15
Requirements	None
Effect	Creates a 'ghost' form that can scout areas.
Tips	When you activate this strange power, a ghostly mental projection is created that can explore areas without revealing its presence to your foes. The psychic projection cannot interact with the real world, but does allow you to safely scout an area ahead.

OBFUSCATE

Generally, the only way to see through the deceptions of the Obfuscate discipline is through powers such as Heightened Senses and Eyes of the Beast. However, characters with very high Perception may penetrate the disguise.

Cloak of Shadows

Blood Cost	5
Requirements	Wits > 25
Effect	Renders your character invisible to normal sight.
Tips	Cloak of Shadows renders your character invisible to mortal sight. It is directly opposed by the disciplines that reveal hidden objects (Heightened Senses, Eyes of the Beast, and True Sight). Whenever Cloak of Shadows is used, it will allow you to remain unseen, unless an opponent is using one of these counter-disciplines. However, if you move or attack, the level of your cloak will degrade by one until it disappears completely.

Mask of A Thousand Faces

Blood Cost	5
Requirements	Wits > 30
Effect	This power allows you to duplicate the appearance of one enemy.
Tips	When you activate this power, your character takes on the 'Seeming' of the target. This means enemies may consider you their friend and not attack you. It is best used to scout out enemy defenses and plan surprise assaults. Your Seeming dissipates when you make an attack or its duration expires.

Cloak the Gathering

Blood Cost	10
Requirements	Wits > 40
Effect	Renders your entire coterie obfuscated.
Tips	This power applies the effects of Cloak of Shadows to your entire coterie, allowing your entire group to move undetected.

DEMENTATION

The mental attacks within the Dementation group are most often resisted by the target's Wits.

Passion

Blood Cost	5
Requirements	Charisma > 25
Effect	Increases the chance of Frenzy in the target.
Tips	This power increases the chance that the target will fall into Frenzy. It is useful for disrupting enemy tactics.

The Haunting

Blood Cost	5
Requirements	Manipulation > 35
Effect	Drives a target to distraction with ghostly images.
Tips	This is most useful for breaking up a coordinated group of enemies. The target of this power will be distracted and unable to act coherently, possibly attacking their allies or wandering off.

Eyes of Chaos

Blood Cost	10
Requirements	Perception > 50
Effect	Reveals the target's aura.
Tips	Like Aura Perception, this power is most useful in multiplayer games.

Voice of Madness

Blood Cost	15
Requirements	Manipulation > 60
Effect	Lowers a target's mental attributes, as well as increasing their Frenzy trait.
Tips	A victim of this discipline is susceptible to other mental assaults, and so it is best used in combination with other disciplines. Use Voice of Madness to lower their resistance, and then add a power such as Possession to seize control of their mind.

DOMINATE

As mental attacks, disciplines within the Dominate group are most often resisted by the target's Wits.

Command

Blood Cost	5
Requirements	Manipulation > 25
Effect	Gives you control over the target for a short period of time.
Tips	This power allows you to control the target as if they were your own character. Although it lasts only a short time, you can wreak havoc by using it to make one enemy attack another. Once they start fighting, they will continue to attack each other, even after your control has expired! You can press the TAB key at any time to return to your body and relinquish control over your victim.

Mesmerize

Blood Cost	10
Requirements	Manipulation > 35
Effect	Makes the target compliant and walk toward you.
Tips	This power is superb in combination with Feed. Not only is the target unable to resist your attack, they will also walk toward you. Be aware that attacking the victim automatically breaks them out of their trance.

The Forgetful Mind

Blood Cost	15
Requirements	Wits > 50
Effect	The target loses the ability to concentrate and will ignore you.
Tips	You can use this power to make enemies ignore you, even after a fight has started. Under the effect of this discipline, they will return to their idle position, unable to concentrate on events around you. They will respond to direct attacks, but will not help their allies, making this an insidious power.

Possession

Blood Cost	20
Requirements	Charisma > 60
Effect	Gives you complete control over the target for an extended period.
Tips	The victim of this discipline loses all conscious control over their actions—you are in charge. It is very similar to Command, save that the effect lasts far longer. You can press the TAB key at any time to return to your body and relinquish control over your victim.

PROTEAN

Eyes of The Beast

Blood Cost	5
Requirements	Perception > 25
Effect	Grants enhanced senses, revealing hidden objects to the caster.
Tips	This power operates exactly like Heightened Senses. Use it to penetrate Invisibility and Cloak of Shadows.

Feral Claws

Blood Cost	5
Requirements	None
Effect	The character grows wicked claws from their hands, which inflict 15 Aggravated damage.
Tips	Feral Claws allows the character to inflict tremendous damage on their opponents. Stamina does not add to soak totals against Aggravated damage, so many enemies are practically helpless against it.

Earth Meld

Blood Cost	10
Requirements	None
Effect	The character fades away into the ground, leaving only a shadow behind.
Tips	Once a character has melded into the earth, enemies will ignore them, making this discipline a great escape route. Also, while resting deep in the earth a character will slowly regenerate health and purge their Frenzy levels. Letting a character rest within the ground is a great way to restore their combat strength. It's slower than Blood Healing, but it can prove cheaper!

Shape of the Beast

Blood Cost	10
Requirements	None
Effect	The character transforms into a wolf!
Tips	Once in wolf form, your character may not use equipment or cast more disciplines. However, the wolf form does grant the advantages of faster movement and Aggravated damage from your claws and bite attack. This is a good way to make an under-equipped character far more ferocious in combat.

Mist Form

Blood Cost	20
Requirements	None
Effect	The character transforms into elemental vapor.
Tips	While in Mist Form, your character is invulnerable attack, although you can still be seen by enemies. You can use this power to scout out dangerous locations and even draw enemies back into a trap while remaining immune to their attacks. Be careful though—elemental attacks and certain high level disciplines may still affect you!

PRESENCE

As mental attacks, disciplines within the Presence group are most often resisted by the target's Wits.

Awe

Blood Cost	5
Requirements	Charisma > 25
Effect	Renders the target compliant and unresisting.
Tips	The victim of this power is unable to resist you, so it is useful for landing the first blow in combat or feeding upon a foe.

Dread Gaze

Blood Cost	5
Requirements	Charisma > 35
Effect	The target of this discipline runs in fear.
Tips	This power causes the target to flee in terror. It is very useful for buying time and removing an opponent from combat temporarily.

Entrancement

Blood Cost	10
Requirements	Appearance > 50
Effect	Renders the target helpless and draws them to you.
Tips	This enhanced form of Awe gives you complete control over the target, allowing you to control them as if they were your own character.

Majesty

Blood Cost	15
Requirements	Appearance > 60
Effect	Creates an aura of power that prevents foes from attacking you.
Tips	Any foe who falls victim to this power, which radiates from your character, is not only drawn to you, but is also rendered incapable of harming you. Large groups of enemies can be instantly neutralized by this power. Attacking an individual within a group of enemies breaks the effect only for that individual; the rest of the group will still be powerless to react.

MORTIS

Shambling Hordes

Blood Cost	5
Requirements	None
Effect	Raises a dead corpse as your temporary servant.
Tips	This allows you to raise the dead as a servant for you character. The targeted dead creature will shamble to its feet and fight for you for a short period of time before collapsing once more. It is useful when you need extra fighters, but the walking dead are not particularly effective fighters.

Vigor Mortis

Blood Cost	10
Requirements	None
Effect	Gives you temporary control over a dead foe.
Tips	This power allows you to control a dead foe, commanding them as if they were your own character. Given that the foe is already dead, and hence especially expendable, it makes sense to use this power for a suicide attack, using the dead to kill your living enemies.

Summon Soul

Blood Cost	15
Requirements	Perception > 50
Effect	Summons a wraith to fight at your side temporarily.
Tips	This power calls a damned soul to your service for a short time. As a spirit, such a servant is deadly in combat and highly resistant to damage, and so can be very efficient at killing your foes. For more details on wraiths, see the *Bestiary* chapter.

Plague Wind

Blood Cost	20
Requirements	Intelligence > 60
Effect	Creates a virulently toxic cloud that damages all within its radius.
Tips	You do not have to target an enemy with this discipline, you can effect an area. This is particularly useful in narrow areas where enemies must pass through the cloud to attack you. In this way, you can hurt many foes with one casting.

Black Death

Blood Cost	25
Requirements	Intelligence > 70
Effect	Strikes a single target with massive damage.
Tips	This power is deadly against a single enemy. Use it when you can spare the blood, or when you have to make sure an enemy is slain— its effects can be tremendous.

BLOOD MAGIC

Blood Rage

Blood Cost	5
Requirements	Intelligence > 25, Wits > 25
Effect	Forces a target to expend their blood pool.
Tips	This power forces a target vampire to burn their blood pool. This is particularly useful against foes who regularly use expensive disciplines, because it will deny them the blood they need to activate their powers.

Blood of Potency

Blood Cost	10
Requirements	None
Effect	Reduces the cost to your character of using disciplines.
Tips	This power is subtle, but highly effective. While it is in effect, all of your disciplines cost less blood to activate, enabling you to use them far more efficiently.

Theft of Vitae

Blood Cost	15
Requirements	Intelligence > 40
Effect	Steals blood from a target and puts it into your blood pool.
Tips	This is a wonderful way to feed from a distance and deny an enemy the use of their blood pool. At low levels, you barely steal back the blood you spent in activating the discipline; at high levels, you can drain a significant portion of the foe's blood into your own pool.

Cauldron of Blood

Blood Cost	20
Requirements	Intelligence > 50
Effect	Ignites the target's blood, inflicting Aggravated damage.
Tips	This spell causes hideous amounts of damage, but that damage is dependent upon the size of a foe's blood pool. Make sure that you use it at the beginning of any encounters so that your foe has not spent their blood casting disciplines on you!

LURE OF FLAMES

Torch

Blood Cost	3
Requirements	Intelligence > 25
Effect	Creates a small ball of bale-fire to illuminate your surroundings.
Tips	The great benefit of this power is that your character no longer needs to use their shield slot for a torch and can equip a shield or two-handed weapon.

Fireball

Blood Cost	5
Requirements	Intelligence > 35
Effect	Projects a ball of fire toward the target.
Tips	The fireball will launch from your character's hands (or more rarely their mouth) and roll toward the target. It may be avoided or it might strike another object along the way, but when it hits, it inflicts Aggravated fire damage to the target.

Flame Ring

Blood Cost	10
Requirements	Intelligence > 60
Effect	Surrounds your character in a halo of flames, damaging all in the immediate area.
Tips	Use this power whenever your character is surrounded by a group of foes. It will damage everyone in the immediate vicinity, quickly clearing up the battlefield. Because the fire is called into existence through will alone, it will not damage your friends.

Immolate

Blood Cost	25
Requirements	Intelligence > 60
Effect	This strikes a single opponent with a blast of fire.
Tips	This spells inflicts great Aggravated fire damage on a single target. Very few beings can resist such an attack, although it is costly to cast.

Firestorm

Blood Cost	20
Requirements	Intelligence > 70
Effect	This blasts an entire area with a rain of fire.
Tips	As you target an area (rather than a person) with this spell, it is useful for attacking entire groups or blocking off narrow corridors. The flames are not greatly damaging individually, but any creature that stays within its area will soon be consumed.

HANDS OF DESTRUCTION

Decay

Blood Cost	5
Requirements	Intelligence > 25, Humanity < 60
Effect	Inflicts Aggravated damage on target.
Tips	This power corrupts the target it attacks, inflicting Aggravated damage. This makes it useful for getting damage past an enemy's resistance.

Acidic Touch

Blood Cost	10
Requirements	Intelligence > 35, Humanity < 50
Effect	Inflicts Aggravated damage on touched target.
Tips	This power inflicts increased damage, but requires that you touch the target (must be in close proximity to the target).

Atrophy

Blood Cost	15
Requirements	Intelligence > 50, Humanity < 35
Effect	Reduces the target's Physical Attributes while inflicting Aggravated damage.
Tips	This nasty power reduces the target's Attributes for an extended period and inflicts Aggravated damage over time. It will slowly wear an enemy down until they are destroyed.

Turn To Dust

Blood Cost	20
Requirements	Intelligence > 60, Humanity < 25
Effect	Inflicts huge amounts of Aggravated damage on target.
Tips	This power blasts a single target with the full power of the blood. This is one of those powers you use when you absolutely must destroy a foe.

BLOOD RITUALS

Heart of Stone

Blood Cost	5
Requirements	Intelligence > 25, Wits > 25
Effect	Protects the character from being staked.
Tips	This wraps the vampire's heart in stone, making it impossible to be staked. It is very useful when fighting foes that regularly use stakes, such as vampire hunters.

Prison of Ice

Blood Cost	10
Requirements	Intelligence > 35, Wits > 35
Effect	Encases the target in ice, freezing them to the spot.
Tips	This power not only damages a target (Aggravated cold), but also renders them immobile. Any foe trapped in the prison can do nothing to escape until the power ends, leaving them vulnerable to repeated attacks.

Call Lightning

Blood Cost	20
Requirements	Intelligence > 50, Wits > 50
Effect	Calls down a blast of lightning upon the target.
Tips	Relying on elemental electricity for damage, this spell bypasses most defenses.

Ignore the Searing Flame

Blood Cost	5
Requirements	Intelligence > 60, Wits > 60
Effect	Increases a character's resistance to Fire damage.
Tips	Once this power is activated, the character's soak total against Fire damage increases tremendously. This is very useful against foes that use flame-based attacks, such as the Tremere.

Summon Elemental

Blood Cost	20
Requirements	Intelligence > 70, Wits > 70
Effect	Summons an Elemental to fight at your side.
Tips	Use this power to turn the odds in your favor. An Elemental is tremendously strong and capable of fighting a number of foes. For more details on Elementals, see the *Bestiary* chapter.

OBTENEBRATION

There are other powers within the Obtenebration group, but only one is demonstrated in Redemption.

Dark Hunter

Blood Cost	20
Requirements	None
Effect	Summons a Dark Hunter into the world to fight at your side.
Tips	Use this power to turn the odds in your favor. As a shadow, a Dark Hunter is resistant to most forms of damage and is a deadly opponent. For more details on Dark Hunters, see the *Bestiary* chapter.

SERPENTIS

Eyes of the Serpent

Blood Cost	5
Requirements	None
Effect	Renders a target insensible and compliant.
Tips	This power is very similar to Mesmerize because it draws a foe to your side and renders them completely vulnerable. Although it is broken if the victim is attacked, it allows you to feed or strike the first blow in combat. Eyes of the Serpent is resisted by the target's Wits attribute.

Tongue of the Asp

Blood Cost	15
Requirements	None
Effect	Steals blood from the target.
Tips	This power is very similar to Theft of Vitae and can be used in exactly the same manner. It steals blood from an opponent and transfers it directly into your blood pool.

Skin of the Adder

Blood Cost	10
Requirements	None
Effect	Provides increased resistance to Aggravated damage.
Tips	When you use this power, your Soak totals against Aggravated damage increase greatly. This gives your character an enhanced chance of survival in combat, especially against foes that use Aggravated or Elemental damage.

Hatch the Viper

Blood Cost	20
Requirements	None
Effect	Summons a viper to fight at your side.
Tips	The viper summoned is small, but its bite is poisonous, which gives it the ability to severely hurt your foes. For more details on vipers, see the *Bestiary* chapter.

NUMINA

The powers of Numina are available only to humans. They are most frequently encountered in multiplayer games amongst vampire hunters and the like.

Invisibility

Mana Cost	5
Requirements	Perception > 25, Intelligence > 25
Effect	Renders your character invisible to normal vision.
Tips	This power works exactly like Cloak of Shadows. It allows human hunters to surprise their vampire foes.

Flash

Mana Cost	10
Requirements	Perception > 35, Intelligence > 35
Effect	Creates a burst of sunlight that blinds and may damage foes.
Tips	When a character activates this power, they are surrounded by a bright flash of light. This can blind or distract opponents and will cause Aggravated damage if they are vulnerable to sunlight, as vampires are.

True Sight

Mana Cost	10
Requirements	Perception > 50, Intelligence > 50
Effect	This grant increases perceptions that pierce Invisibility and Obfuscate.
Tips	This power is identical to Heightened Senses. Use it to detect hidden foes.

FAITH

Faith powers are available only to humans; the Damned can only fear them.

Heal

Mana Cost	5
Requirements	Faith > 25
Effect	Restores the character's health by 5 points per level.
Tips	This is practically identical to Blood Healing, except that it draws on Mana and the power of Faith.

Prayer

Mana Cost	10
Requirements	Faith > 35
Effect	Damages a single 'unholy' target.
Tips	By invoking the power of their faith, a human hunter can damn a single unholy target. Although the definition of 'unholy' varies from hunter to hunter, it certainly includes vampires.

True Faith

Mana Cost	20
Requirements	Faith > 50
Effect	Creates a sanctified aura that damages all unholy beings that approach.
Tips	This power surrounds the character in a holy aura. All unholy beings that enter or remain in the area suffer Aggravated Faith damage.

Multiplayer Hints and Tips

Vampire: The Masquerade - Redemption is a big game that can seem overwhelming at first. These hints and tips look at the multiplayer aspect of the game from the perspective of both players and the Storyteller, which should be useful in getting you started. These guidelines have been assembled from the experiences of the Activision test team.

There are no secrets in the Storyteller section, so feel free to read it even if you primarily want to enjoy the game as a player.

For Players

If you've played other computer role-playing games before, you will find much that is familiar in this one. The basics of spending experience points, keeping track of health, and managing a 'paper-doll' inventory should all be relatively straightforward.

The core differences lie in the graphical richness of the game and the fact that you are not playing a hero, but rather one of the creatures of the night, a childe of Caine, a vampire!

Character Creation

The first thing you should do is choose a character model and decide on a name. Although you can get as crazy as you want, think about the sort of game you want to play in—Storytelling and role-playing chronicles require more serious and realistic names than do simple combat sessions. The character model should be one you like, and one that fits the time period of the chronicle (Medieval or Modern). This is not only to maintain a consistent world, but characters from different time periods will not display each other's arms and equipment accurately.

With only 5000 XP to spend, your character will start out weak and unequipped. To maximize your survival chances, it's a good idea to make your character choices very carefully. Your clan determines which disciplines (vampire powers) you will have access to. With the small amount of points you have at the start of a game, you should specialize in a just a few abilities and perhaps one or two low-level disciplines. By increasing your physical attributes you can be more effective in combat, especially when supported by disciplines such as Blood Healing and Potence. If you increase your social attributes and buy disciplines such as Dominate or Presence, you can use these powers to control the enemy without actually getting directly into the fight yourself. You can even be a sorcerer, using the powers of blood magic (thaumaturgy) or necromancy (mortis) to overwhelm your foes.

The effectiveness of your vampiric powers is calculated by combining one of your attributes with the power level of the specific discipline. Therefore, it's best to concentrate your points at this stage of the game. As the game progresses and you earn more experience, feel free to expand. If your Storyteller is feeling generous, they can grant you additional experience and discipline groups in order to play at a more powerful level.

You cannot purchase equipment for your character during character creation, so you will have to wait for the game to start before you can arm yourself. Your Storyteller should help you equip your character, especially if there are plans for a particularly dangerous adventure.

A Small Note on Cheating

Most online role-playing games severely restrict the ability to cheat (to grant your character items and powers he has not earned). *Vampire: The Masquerade - Redemption* is different. Because of the power given to Storytellers, it is perfectly possible to take your favorite character into a game in which you are the Storyteller and grant yourself every magical object, maximum abilities, and all of the disciplines at maximum level. The question you should ask yourself is, "What does all this power get me?" The answer is very little. If a Storyteller does not approve of your character, they can kick you from a game—they can even kill you with a simple command—so all of your abilities cannot protect you.

A fully equipped character with maxed-out abilities is virtually invulnerable, so there would be little challenge in playing such a character and no way that a Storyteller could create a feasible story for such a monster. In short, you probably would not be able to find a chronicle that would be satisfying if you did this to your character. Our advice is to let your character grow slowly as your adventure unfolds and not abuse the system. (Of course, you should create one maxed-out character just to see what you can do, and then put that character to rest after having your fun!)

Some General Advice

As a player, you should aim to have fun in the game, but not at the expense of the other participants. This game does not allow player vs. player conflict and gives great power to the Storyteller, so it pays to be nice—there are no rewards for being bad!

- **Be courteous.** Your Storyteller may be as new to the game as you are. If he is busy when you request help, wait patiently. Don't make constant demands.

- **Ask first.** Find out if your character is suitable for the game you want to join. If your character has any odd items (magic weapons, rare objects), then check with your Storyteller to see if she will allow you to use them. If she will not, don't use them in the game—the Storyteller could take them away from you if she felt so inclined. Also make sure that your character matches the time period. Many Storytellers will not allow anachronistic characters into their games.

Some Things to Look Out For

- **Loading times:** The first time anyone enters a new area, first the Storyteller and then the character who made the transition will notice that the 'LOADING' window will appear. While the host is loading a zone, the game is effectively paused, so don't worry if everything seems to stop for a moment. The Storyteller can also pause the game, in which case he will be able to explain his own reasons for doing so.

- **Possession:** The Storyteller may take control of your character, though she should warn you if they are about to do it. If this happens, there is probably a good reason, so go along for the ride.

- **Animation freeze:** If the data is interrupted as it is sent from your computer to the host, your character may appear to be locked in one pose. In this case, do something that forces a new animation on your character: Use a discipline, get involved in combat, etc.

Q&A

Q *The game keeps on pausing. What's happening?*

A Whenever the Storyteller's system is busy, the game will pause for a moment. This occurs when a new area is being loaded, or if the Storyteller is fiddling with some of the game's options. Storytellers may also pause the game if they need to pay attention to, or arrange, a specific event. If these pauses are interfering with gameplay too much, inquire with the Storyteller.

Q *Why is the game so hard or so easy?*

A Whereas the single player (SP) game is carefully balanced so that the individual dungeon will always match your character's abilities, the multiplayer (MP) game is far more open-ended. The difficulty of the two core MP chronicles could be considered mid-range, so that starting characters can easily be swept aside by the opposition, but experienced and well-equipped characters will find no challenge. The Storyteller should adjust the level of opposition by adding or removing enemies to make the area challenging, but not impossible, to the players.

Q *Why can't I control my character?*

A The Storyteller has the ability to possess your character, in which case he will control your character's actions, rather than you. If this happens, the Storyteller should have a reason for his actions. Ask for an explanation. Also, if your character is in frenzy or under the influence of an enemy's discipline, you may lose control for a short time (look for icons appearing in the lower-right corner of the game window).

Q *I tried that and I still can't move where I want to!*

A A couple of things could be happening. First, your Storyteller can move around the game invisibly (as the Floating Head o' Doom). She may be standing where you want to go and, hence, blocking your movement. Also several NPCs can make themselves invisible and may also be blocking your path.

Q *I just started a game and my equipment is missing!*

A Two things could have happened. The first is that your character might not have been saved because you did not exit the game properly. If your computer crashed or shutdown during the game, then character data may be lost. Secondly, it is possible that you have the equipment, but it is not appearing on your character model. Open your inventory and re-equip everything; it should now appear.

Q *I don't like my Storyteller! He sucks!*

A Find a Storyteller that suits your style of play, or run a game yourself. *VTM: Redemption* supports a wide variety of play styles, so you should have no difficulty finding a game that appeals to you. Chat in the Lobby to find people who share similar gaming styles and remember their names when you next seek a game.

Q *Why is this game different from the pen-and-paper game?*

A *VTM: Redemption* is an adaptation of the pen-and-paper game. Just as a novel is not the same as a movie, the medium of computer games necessitates changes to how things work. The changes were made to create a better game while remaining as true as possible to the license. This also explains why not every clan, bloodline, and permutation of the PnP game is in *VTM: Redemption*. Should you want a character type that is not available in this game talk to your ST, there may well be ways of treating your character as if he had the desired attributes without needing drastic changes in the game. For example, if you wanted to use your PnP character that has the merit of Misplaced Heart (rendering him less vulnerable to staking) your Storyteller could use his control over the game to simulate the merit by 'un-staking' you if were staked.

For Storytellers

Storytelling is both the most innovative and the hardest part of the game. Without a doubt, a lot of responsibility rests on your shoulders and it may take you a while to get used to your role.

Initially, the sheer range of options you have at your disposal seems daunting; however, most of the options can be broken down into how you respond to players' actions and, hence, become simpler.

The best way to begin to understand the tools at your disposal is to go into a game without players and just experiment with the buttons. Whenever you create or delete an object, possess an NPC, or teleport about the map, think about how these actions will help you to run a better game. Work out the limitations of your control over the environment and learn how to maximize your efficiency. These initial solo forays into the game world will provide the basis for all of your later skills as a Storyteller.

The Buttons

Your main controls are a series of panes that you can open to alter various aspects of the game. A cluster of buttons on the left of the screen control aspects of characters and objects, while the buttons to the right of the text window bring up the information panes, and the buttons on the far right of the screen set other functions.

The buttons on the left of the screen near your character portrait give you control over an Actor (PC or NPC) in the game. Once you have selected a character using the Actors Pane, or by clicking on them in Storyteller mode, you have the following options:

- **Possess:** This allows you to take over the character and move him as you would your own body.

- **Revive:** This button acts like the discipline effect Awaken, restoring a vampire in torpor to life. This tool only works on player characters, not NPCs.

- **AI Setting:** This toggles between Talk (when the talk cursor appears over them, they cannot be damaged), Neutral (no special cursor, but not a fighting character), and Attack (the character is combative and can take and receive damage). This allows you to define NPCs as enemies or friends. Any character that you intend to use to interact with the PCs should be set to Talk so they cannot be attacked. Even the main villain (if you have one) should be set to talk mode so he cannot be attacked until you are ready; possess him, cackle maniacally, then set him to attack mode!

- **Delete:** This will remove the object, prop, or actor you have selected from the world. It will not affect player characters. Your Storyteller Head immediately replaces the object you delete.

- **Character Mode:** This takes you out of Storyteller mode and into Character mode. In Character mode you lose all of your special tools and act just like a normal character in the game. To be able to attack players with an NPC you control, you will have to go into Character mode. Likewise you can only pick up objects in Character mode. A button under your character portrait will return you to Storyteller mode.

The panes you can open are:

- **Location:** This pane lists all of the areas in the game. The one marked with the asterisk (*) represents the current location of your character's body. You can easily teleport from one location to another to keep up with the action. The information bought up by other panes (for example, the Actors Pane) refers to the highlighted location. If you need access to a different part of the map, teleport over there!

- **Objects:** This pane allows you to add things to the world. The buttons on the right of the list separate the list into actors (NPCs that can move and fight), objects (equipment and other things characters can pick up), and props (the background details of the setting). Be careful when placing props so that you don't block off areas of the map—some of the props are fairly large!

- **Scene:** The pre-scripted scenes that advance the story are displayed here. You can use the controls to skip the story forward as if events had been triggered in game. For example, one of the triggers in *To Curse The Darkness* is a meeting with the Nosferatu Melmoth. If you decided to play out the conversation yourself, you would disable the cutscene and then use the Scenes control to advance the story after the players had talked to him. The Scene controls are probably the most complicated tool that you have access to; use it with care until you are certain of what you're doing.

- **Controls:** These controls affect the games as a whole, showing the time you have been playing and allowing you to kick or bar players from the game. You should consider locking your game to outside chat if you plan on role-playing serious conversations that require everyone's attention.

- **Actors:** This window lists all the characters (NPCs and PCs) in your current zone. By using the controls, you can quickly jump between them, possess them, or change their mode. These are, in fact, the same controls that appear at the left-hand side of the screen. The actor's health is also listed, which can be very useful in keeping track of fight scenes.

Finally there are three buttons on the far right of the screen:

- **Pause:** This pauses the game, preventing movement until you restart things. This is good to use if you need to take time to assess a situation. Tell your players that you have paused the game, otherwise expect a lot of chat messages asking you what's happening!

- **Head:** This launches the Storyteller Head, which is invisible to the players and invulnerable. It can be used to place objects and enemies without worry.

- **Advancement:** This brings up the Character Advancement window for all players in the game, starting with your own character. By clicking on the cross next to the Earned Experience box, you can grant players the experience points you feel they deserve. Click OK to proceed to each player in turn. Once you have made your selections, the Advancement window will open for each player, allowing them to spend the XP you gave them. When the Advancement window is open, you can spend the points for the players if you feel that they need a specific ability in the game. You can do this in the same way as character creation by clicking on the crosses next to attributes or disciplines to spend the points.

By combining the various buttons and information panes, you have fairly complete control over the game environment. For your first games, it would probably be best to use only the most basic control. Use the Objects Pane to equip the coterie with basic weapons and armor; use the Actors Pane to remove some of the enemies to give the players an easier time. Once you have the grasp of the basics, begin to influence the game more. Possess an NPC and talk to the PCs, invent an extra quest for them and create new enemies for them to fight, use the Location Pane to teleport deep into the level, and create unexpected monsters for the coterie to encounter.

Once you are certain of the controls, load up one of the empty maps, block off any of the doors that you don't want the players to go through, and start creating encounters for them. (By using the editing tools outside of the game, you can create your own chronicles by linking only the areas you need together, but for now just blocking the doors you don't want the coterie to open will suffice!)

Think about how different enemies will challenge the coterie and plan their location. For instance, enemies with missile weapons in an area that the PCs cannot easily reach, a swarm of little creatures in a narrow space where the characters cannot maneuver easily, or a wide open space where invisible enemies can easily hide! The possibilities are endless.

Don't forget to put in some NPCs that you can possess to talk to the players and give them information, quests, or equipment. Remember the poor civilians too, so the PCs have someone to feed from.

Some Things to Look Out For

- **Loading Times:** The first time anyone enters a new area, first the Storyteller and then the character who made the transition will notice that the 'LOADING' window will appear. While the host is loading a zone, the game is effectively paused so your players may be momentarily confused. Also, you can be distracted by the 'LOADING' window if a PC makes a transition into a zone you have not loaded, so be prepared for this if everyone is running through the game rapidly!

- **Possession Lag:** If you possess a player character, then that player will have no control over their actions. This possession ends only when you move into another body—sometimes you forget to let go of the PC, which can be deeply frustrating for them. After possessing a player character, always go into another body (or your Glowing Head o' Doom) and possess it. This will ensure that the PC is now free to continue.

- **What am I?** When you're in Storyteller mode, objects are highlighted as you pass the cursor over them. If you click the mouse button, your camera centers on that object and it becomes selected for you. It's very easy to think you're moving your character when you suddenly click on an object—the door, a table, or a fireplace—and become confused. If you're not sure where you are, use the TAB key to switch between the characters in the game or bring up the Actors Pane. You can also call up the Storyteller Head and use that to re-center yourself. Pressing the Character Mode button will also take you into the last character you possessed, as well as taking you out of Storyteller mode.

- **Where's the Door?** It is possible for you to use your Storyteller powers to break the game. The most common example of this is in deleting a vital object or actor from the game. For example, if you delete the door that leads into a new zone, it will be impossible to make that transition. Don't worry if you do this, just remember not to do it next time. Without restricting a Storyteller's power too much, situations like this are unavoidable!

Some Shortcuts

- **Console commands:** In addition to all the buttons and panes, the Storyteller can directly enter commands into the game console. Sometimes this is quicker than using the buttons. You can bring up the console by hitting the tilde key (~) at the top-left of your keyboard. The most useful commands that you can use here would be:

  Addthing {name}: Adds the named thing (object, prop, or actor) to your location.

  Revive: Same as the revive arrow. Raises a character from torpor.

  Jump {location}: Moves all characters (ST and PCs) to named location. Use this one with care as it can upset the flow of the story.

There are many other console commands, but these three are very good shortcuts for a Storyteller to know. 'Addthing' is perhaps the most useful as it allows you to add objects to the game world without scrolling through the object list. You can create an instant enemy or reward to spice things up. 'Addthing werewolf' is not recommended for starting coteries!

226

- **Short port:** As the Storyteller, you not only have the ability to jump between areas (using the Locations Pane), but also within an area. By using the ALT key and right-clicking the mouse, you are instantly teleported to the place where the cursor is pointing. Be advised that this can put you in an area where your character cannot move or is otherwise stuck—you may have to teleport to get out. This power is most useful when you are in Head mode. Select a place that a character normally cannot reach, a tabletop for instance, and use the teleport power to reach it. Now create an object—it will appear on top of the table rather than on the floor!

How to Be a Good Storyteller

There are so many different styles of play that it would be unreasonable to suggest how to create a story. Instead, we'll focus on how to use the game's tools to their best advantage. With the tools at your disposal you can create any style of game—from Anarchy hack-and-slash, to Elysium political role-playing. The tools remain the same, it is merely the use to which they are put!

When a player you don't know enters your game, take a minute to look at their character—possess the character and then go into Character mode. Look at their attributes, disciplines, and equipment. If you see anything you don't like, inform the player of your concerns. Remember, it is your responsibility to make the game fun and interesting, and a character that is too powerful could easily disrupt that for everyone else.

If everyone is playing a new character, you should probably help them out a little. Provide some basic equipment and even some experience points if you feel your game is going to be a tough one. Do not give out too much free experience, as it cheapens the rewards for actually playing—5000 extra points gives the character a significant boost at the beginning of the game! Good equipment for a starting medieval character is:

- Leather or Padded Armor
- Broadsword or Mace and Shield or Halberd
- 2 Bottles of Vitae

And for a modern character would be:

- Leather jacket
- Pistol or shotgun
- 2 Bottles of Vitae

If you are going to be running a really tough game, feel free to increase the goodies that you are giving out. Also, players may request specific items that fit their character design. Give out scythes and scimitars instead of the broadsword, but don't let them convince you they need the Ivory Bow or Ainkurn Sword from the start of the game!

You can also play cooperatively with the other players by staying in Character mode. Use your Storyteller powers only at the beginning of the game if anyone needs equipment or help, but after that stay in character. You can call on the Storyteller tools anytime you need them, but otherwise you will be just like any other character in the game.

Finally, you should pay attention to the basics to stay on top of your game.

- **Know Where the PCs are.** Use the TAB key to check up on all of the players. Just because someone is being quiet does not mean you shouldn't monitor him.

- **Pay attention.** If several people are talking at once, the text window can fill up and scroll rapidly. Pay attention so that you know if a player needs your intervention, or wants to initiate a conversation with an NPC. If you think you missed something, use the scroll bar to check.

- **Provide fair rewards.** If you throw strong enemies at the players, they have the right to expect rewards either in the form of treasure or experience. Be fair, and reward them for doing well.

- **You're the boss.** This is a very important rule. You have absolute power and within the game you are in charge. Don't abuse that power, but don't let anyone walk all over you either. It's your game!

Q&A

Q *Why must I have a character to host a game?*

A The short answer is so that you have a presence in the system—a 'body' from which to chat. The longer answer would be because it is often useful for you to have a default presence within the game world. Rather than seeing your character as a hindrance, explore its uses. You have a mouthpiece for giving information to the players, and you have a character that can aid the coterie, dispense items, or lead the way through a puzzle. The floating head and camera modes allow you access to the game in ways the PCs cannot, and the character mode allows you to see what the game is like from the ground.

Q *Why can't I zone as an NPC or as the Glowing Head o' Doom?*

A So the system can keep track of where you are (i.e., which area of the game you want to affect). Your original body is considered to be where you are. As such, you cannot make a transition inside another character. With the location pane controls at your command, you can easily move your original body into a new zone to catch up with the action. If you want to affect a different zone, then move the camera (using the TAB key) to a PC you want to follow and possess a character or create a Storyteller Head at that point. You can add or delete things from that viewpoint without needing your body along for the ride.

Q *I wanted to talk to the PCs in character, but the text shows up as 'Storyteller says'?*

A Unless you possess a body, you are assumed to be the ST. To talk in character, jump to that actor (using the Actor Pane or just clicking on them when in Storyteller mode) and press the Possess button. Now you can talk and move as that character, and even go into full Character mode if you need to!

Q *I possessed an NPC, but he kept on moving by himself. What's happening?*

A If the actor that you possess is in frenzy, fear mode, or under the influence of mind-controlling disciplines, you will not have full control over them until the effect ends.

Q *NPCs won't attack me; they just follow my character around!*

A The character settings (Talk/Neutral/Attack) affect your character, as well as NPCs. Unless you are set to Attack, you are not considered a target. If you want to use your character in a game (playing cooperatively with the other players), make sure you are set to Attack mode!

Some Ideas

These are fun things we have been able to do with the game. Try them out, expand upon them, and see where your imagination takes you!

The Not-So-Nice Un-alive II

If you translate the title you'll decipher the name to a popular movie, which involves zombies, skeletons, and modern weapons in the Dark Ages. This sort of thing can be a lot of fun. Allow the players to create modern characters and give them some standard equipment, such as shotguns and chainsaws (look in the objects list), but do not give them too much ammunition. Create several packs of skeletons and zombu (look for them in the actors list) and scatter them liberally around the area. Tell the players to take their 'boom-sticks' and clean out the town.

Any player who can remember quotes from the movie (or any other appropriate movie) should be awarded bonus experience or ammunition!

For added spice, create a medium tough monster and possess it yourself, then wander the world hunting the hapless coterie down! Remember to shout "Braaaainss!" a lot when possessing the zombies!

Blood Fury

Set up the game normally, but make sure that there are very few blood sources in the game—no civilians, no easy-to-feed-upon enemies, and a shortage of Vitae Vials. Choose monsters that either have no blood (wraiths or spiders, for example) or are protected from being fanged (Teutonic Knights in full armor!).

The game will start off normally, but fairly soon the coterie will realize that they are running low on blood. This means that they cannot use their disciplines and will frenzy far more often. Watch them start to feed on one another as the panic sets in and the tougher enemy bosses close in for the kill.

The Preset Chronicles

Vampire: The Masquerade—Redemption comes with two pre-designed multiplayer chronicles (*To Curse the Darkness* and *Leaves of Three*), as well as four empty maps and three saloons (virtual chat rooms). The empty maps, which correspond to each of the major hubs in the single player game, are there for you to populate and design your own adventures; the saloons are designed as virtual chat rooms where you can interact in character. The two chronicles represent pre-designed adventures, which you can run through with little alteration, or customize as much as you want!

The details of the chronicles presented here give you the basic information—enough to find your way around and the bare-bones of the plot. This is because your Storyteller can alter any facet of the chronicle and thus any information presented here could be invalid for the game you are playing. The details here should help you, but expect some surprises!

To Curse the Darkness

This chronicle takes place in the Dark Ages, in a small village in Eastern Europe called Temesvar. The adventure starts with the coterie being forced to stop their journey because of the presence of moonbeasts (werewolves) in the area.

Plot Overview

The coterie discovers that the village of Temesvar is cursed—there have been fires, thefts, and a mysterious wasting sickness is afflicting the inhabitants. By talking to the people of the town, the players will discover that there is a conflict between two powerful vampires—Melmoth and LeComte—and that the leader of the village's Nosferatu has recently been killed. Talking to the NPCs leads to conflicting accounts of what has happened and the coterie has no choice but to venture into the Nosferatu tunnels to discover the truth!

Leaving the Inn, the players are confronted by a starving Cainite who is revealed to be Melmoth, a crippled Nosferatu. Following him to his haven, the players will agree to help him regain his stolen property—the Monocle of Clarity—in exchange for his help in leaving town. Moving through the village streets, the coterie will encounter several humans who can help fill in plot details. They may come to suspect that Melmoth is lying to them, but they have no choice but to enter the Nosferatu tunnels to find the Toreador, LeComte.

After fighting their way past the leaderless Nosferatu, the coterie emerges into the crypts beneath the church where they find the missing stableboy, Ragwick. He can answer many of the coterie's questions and lead them to LeComte. The artistic Toreador is studying painting in a secret haven within the church itself—he uses the Monocle to discern the hidden details in Cainite paintings and is loath to give it up, although he can be convinced to do so.

Returning through the tunnels with the Monocle, the coterie may find a secret room where the village's stolen Reliquary rests. Taking this to Mother Eglantine should help assuage the villagers' fears.

Finally, the coterie can return to Melmoth's haven and confront the Nosferatu. He plans treachery, so there is one last fight before the quest ends. If the coterie is successful they not only have the Monocle of Clarity, but two new servants—Ragwick and Rebecca—who can help them leave the village and pass through the werewolves' territory!

Geography

Temesvar uses the map of the North Quarter in Prague and Josef's Tunnels. The enemies and secrets the coterie face are identical to those of the single player game. Read the section of the walkthrough on Josef's Tunnels to learn your way around the map and for tips on how to fight the resident Nosferatu.

Many NPCs have been added to the map, ranging from the hapless townsfolk (Mother Eglantine, Sheriff Blazaj, Rebecca, Sorvena, and Udolpho) to the Cainite enemies (Melmoth and LeComte). Each of these NPCs has their own view on what is happening in the village and you should pay careful attention to what they say.

Tips

Both Melmoth and LeComte are elder vampires, fully versed in their clan disciplines. You should use caution fighting them and it may be wiser to negotiate (depending on what your Storyteller decides to allow).

When fighting the Nosferatu in the tunnels, remember to stick together. Lone characters can easily be overpowered and you are stronger as a team.

Leaves of Three

Leaves of Three is set in the modern nights during a turbulent period of Kindred history. The embattled Camarilla is organizing its defense of New York City as the Sabbat try to wipe out their last refuge. There is quite a lot of politics in this chronicle and it can be confusing if you are not familiar with the World of Darkness. If you do know the World of Darkness, you may discover some secrets that could surprise you!

Plot Overview

The coterie are New York supporters of the Camarilla assigned to provide security at an important meeting in the Barclay Hotel. They will meet many powerful NPCs who represent the elders of the Camarilla in New York City and listen to their plans against the Sabbat.

The players start in the lobby of the Barclay Hotel. They should talk to Bill Campbell and Dominic, and then go into their haven. (Returning to the haven represents the passing of time in this chronicle; hence, it advances the plot to the next scene!) The next night, the members of New York's Primogen enter the hotel where they are greeted and taken to their rooms. In the next scene, the coterie watches the Primogen arguing over their next course of action. Retiring to their havens as dawn comes, everyone is met by a grisly sight as night falls. The Brujah representative has been murdered and the coterie is accused of the crime and found guilty in short order.

The punishment for the crime is to be exposed to the sun in a specially designed, inescapable chamber on the top floor of Dominic's factory complex. The adventure begins! Bill, who voices his distrust of Dominic, frees the coterie from the trap—they must not only escape, but also clear their names!

The players fight their way through the factory and escape onto the streets of New York. They should take the taxi to the docks area and search for Dominic's secret meeting place (a new location under Dev/Null's apartment). There they overhear a conversation between Dominic and the Triplets. The Triplets are perfectly happy to betray Dominic to the players and send them on a quest to retrieve the Blood Pact. The Triplets give the coterie access to a hidden haven—in the same location as Dev's apartment!

To find the information they need, the coterie must return to uptown, avoiding the packs of vampires searching for them, and confront Dominic's servant, Luke. Luke fills in more details of Dominic's plan and sends then to the Malkavian warehouse to find the pact. The warehouse is in the dock's area and presents a tough fight—Malkavians combine the worst aspects of the Ventrue and the Nosferatu (invisibility and mind-control) with a dash of homicidal mania for good measure.

Finding the Blood Pact and returning to the Triplets, the coterie can either surrender the pact (losing a good chance of proving their innocence) or try to return to the Barclay Hotel. The only way to avoid the now intensive search for them is to descend into the sewers and fight their way past the Nosferatu to enter the Barclay through a secret entrance.

The end of the chronicle involves the coterie trying to clear their names and prove Dominic's guilt in the form of the Primogen and a Camarilla justicar, Lucinde! If they have found enough evidence, they are successful; if not, they will be branded as traitors and destroyed.

Geography

This chronicle uses the New York map—including Orsi's Factory, the Giovanni Warehouse, and the Sewers. These locations have been subtly changed so that you'll face somewhat different enemies. The biggest change is that the warehouse is not Alesandro's stronghold, but rather the lair of a brood of Sabbat Malkavians. The sewers connect to the Barclay Hotel instead of opening onto the streets of uptown New York.

Also, you must fight through the Factory backward (from the top down), which may be confusing if you're used to the single player map.

Tips

This is a long and involved chronicle. You may not be able to finish it in one sitting, but your Storyteller can save the game so that you can pick up where you left off.

The coterie will face many enemies who use modern weapons, so all the tips from the single player section about facing down firearms apply here. The biggest danger to watch for is friendly fire—your teammates may get trigger-happy and prove as dangerous as your enemies.

Fighting Malkavians is insanely dangerous. They combine the mind control of the Ventrue with the invisibility of the Nosferatu. The Kooks have a love of misdirection, powerful firearms, and torturing their foes. Be very, very careful fighting your way through their warehouse stronghold!